Lonergan on Conversion

American University Studies

Series VII
Theology and Religion

Vol. 124

PETER LANG
New York • San Francisco • Bern • Baltimore
Frankfurt am Main • Berlin • Wien • Paris

Mary Kay Kinberger

Lonergan on Conversion

Applications for Religious Formation

PETER LANG
New York • San Francisco • Bern • Baltimore
Frankfurt am Main • Berlin • Wien • Paris

Library of Congress Cataloging-in-Publication Data

Kinberger, Mary Kay.
   Lonergan on conversion : applications for religious formation /
Mary Kay Kinberger.
     p. cm. — (American university studies. Series VII, Theology and
religion ; v. 124)
   Includes bibliographical references .
   1. Lonergan, Bernard J. F.—Contributions in concept of conversion.
2. Conversion—History of doctrines—20th century.   I. Title.   II. Series.
BV4916.K46   1992   248.8′9425—dc20   91-31788
ISBN 0-8204-1743-2   CIP
ISSN 0740-0446

Die Deutsche Bibliothek-CIP-Einheitsaufnahme

Kinberger, Mary Kay:
Lonergan and conversion : applications for religious formation /
Mary Kay Kinberger.—New York; Berlin; Bern; Frankfurt/M.; Paris;
Wien; Lang, 1992
   (American university studies : Ser. 7, Theology and religion ;
Vol. 124)
     ISBN 0-8204-1743-2
NE: American university studies/07

The paper in this book meets the guidelines for permanence and
durability of the Committee on Production Guidelines for
Book Longevity of the Council on Library Resources.

© Peter Lang Publishing, Inc., New York 1992

Printed in the United States of America.

Acknowledgements

Some people have a dream, but keep that dream tightly sealed in a little box within themselves. Those who have the courage to take the dream out of the box have extraordinary friends who also believe in their dream. Cynthia Knowles, M.S.C. has been that special person for me! She listened to my dream and encouraged me to free the dream from its box and to allow it to take flight! Thank you, Cynthia, for your faith-filled presence in my life!

I am appreciative to the administration of my religious congregation, the Marianites of Holy Cross, for affording me the time and space to pursue doctoral studies.

There are many people who have supported me along this journey. A few of the significant ones include: my parents; my brother and sisters and their families; the members of my religious congregation; Nancy and Bill Burnett; Hazel Ford; the Holy Name sisters at Marian Hall in Spokane, Washington; and my present colleagues at the Catholic Life Center in the Diocese of Baton Rouge, Louisiana. You have encouraged Katie's flight by the gift of your friendship!

I am indebted to Sr. Peggy Nichols, C.S.J. and the National Board of the Religious Formation Conference who gave me the opportunity to present the questionnaire at the National Formation Congress in October, 1987.

Michael Rende, a professor in the Religious Studies Department at Gonzaga University, was a tremendous support to me in the development of the theoretical framework for this study. His willingness to share with me his knowledge, expertise, and understanding of Bernard Lonergan's theology enabled this project to come to fruition.

During my doctoral study, I was blessed with the marvelous opportunity of working with Dr. Richard Wolfe as his graduate assistant. His creed is manifested in his deeds; he shapes the theory of educational leadership into a living reality!

Without the challenging assistance and encouraging support from my dissertation committee, Dr. Patrick J. Ford, S.J., Dr. Richard O. Wolfe, and Dr. Sandra M. Wilson, this study would not have been actualized. I am especially grateful to each of you for being Katie's compass and guide as she spread her wings and took flight!

Dedication

This book is gratefully dedicated

to my loving parents

— Bob and Sis Kinberger —

who have given me

life, roots, and wings to fly!

Table of Contents

Lonergan on Conversion

Chapter One

Lonergan on Conversion: Applications for Religious Formation

Prologue

On a sunny and breezy Sunday afternoon, Katie spread her wings and flew over the Pacific coast where the ocean meets the jagged cliffs. The day was bright with blue, cloudless skies and the air currents were strong enough to offer Katie a relaxed and invigorating flight. As she soared, she met two fellow eagles. "Where are you going this lovely, summer afternoon?" she asked. "We are off to join a novitiate group that emphasizes spiritual growth and development. Their novitiate is even located in the congregation's house of prayer!" Katie thought for a moment and then responded, "Well, I certainly wish you all the best. Hope that you find the spiritual development for which you are searching."

Katie continued her flight and soon encountered another eagle. "How are you doing on this gorgeous day?" she asked. The eagle responded: "I am doing great! I am on my way to join a novitiate group that emphasizes psychosocial development. I have heard that when you finish this program you really have it all together!" As she wished good luck to the young eagle, Katie thought to herself that it certainly would be wonderful to have her own life together.

Katie continued to soar on the warm air currents and soon came upon two more eagles. They greeted one another and the eagles told Katie that they were about to join a novitiate group that emphasized peace and justice. Katie responded: "Well, peace and justice certainly are needed in our troubled world. I hope your expectations are met!"

Katie was now perplexed. What had begun as a pleasant, relaxing flight had left her filled with wonder, and with many unanswered questions. She alighted at the top of a huge pine tree overlooking the Pacific Ocean. She thought to herself, "All the eagles I met this afternoon are going to join novitiate groups that seem to have really important agendas, but something is puzzling me about each novitiate." The wind had increased in its intensity and although the branch to which she clung moved with the steady breeze, she noticed that there was a stability in the entire tree. As she glanced down toward the bottom of the tree she noticed that the roots of the tree intertwined themselves around the rocks and embedded themselves into the earth below. The rocks and the earth formed the foundation for the tree and gave the tree strength to withstand the changing wind currents that daily buffeted it.

This observation made Katie realize what was baffling her about these programs. Although each program focused on important issues, what was the foundation from which they drew their raison d'etre? What supplied the rocks and the earth to each program and provided rootedness for the program?

Katie decided she would have to do some further investigation into these questions before she could satisfy herself with some answers. Thus began Katie's search for a foundation for the novitiate experience in religious congregations.

Come join Katie as she describes her journey. . . .

Description of the Problem

Religious life, as a dynamic, living reality, is characterized by the paschal rhythm of birth, death, and resurrection. This paschal rhythm has been very evident since the Second Vatican Council mandated a renewal of religious life over twenty-five years ago in the document, *Perfectae Caritatis*: "The appropriate renewal of religious life involves two simultaneous processes: a continuous return to the sources of all Christian life and to the original inspiration behind a given community; and an adjustment of the community to the changed conditions of the times. . . . This renewal should go forward under the influence of the Holy Spirit and the guidance of the Church."[1]

Through the mandate of *Perfectae Caritatis*, religious were called upon to renew their gospel vision of Jesus. This vision was to be shaped by the spirit of their founders and the sound traditions of the heritage and charism of their congregations. In light of the gospel vision of Jesus Christ, religious were to adapt their congregations' expressions of this Spirit-given charism and identity to the world that was emerging.[2]

Following the directions of this Council and in obedience to subsequent papal documents, enormous efforts were made to renew and adapt religious life. However, the call of *Perfectae Caritatis* was often not actualized because renewal was seen as external change rather than internal transformation.[3] Indeed, for many religious the degree of inner renewal was measured by the number of exterior alterations. The Council had envisioned that updating these structures would be a first step in a metamorphosis and would result in deep interior renewal. However, external modifications were not always reflective of internal reformation.[4]

This tremendous enterprise of renewal was not without a price. One of the staggering aspects of this cost was the numerical erosion of religious congregations.[5] Gradually the romantic euphoria of religious during and after Vatican II gave way to depression in many of the members. External adaptations did not automatically bring authentic revitalization. Some, seeing their hopes obliterated, decided to seek a meaningful life outside their religious congregations. Others departed from their congregations for diverse reasons, and the result was an unprecedented exodus of thousands of religious.[6]

Consequently since 1966 the number of religious women has decreased from 181,421 to 121,370. The number of religious brothers has dropped to slightly over 60% of what it was prior to 1966. Although the number of religious priests has remained about the same since 1966, fewer young men are now entering the seminaries so their numbers also will decrease over time.[7]

Along with the departure of large numbers, there has been a great decline in the number of people entering religious life. The United States has been especially affected. Where novitiate classes had been comprised of twenty to thirty novices in the sixties, now there are two to three, if any at all. Throughout the United States, convents and institutions have closed, and the average age of the sisters has steadily increased.[8]

The problem of decreased numbers of vocations is closely linked to the question of initial formation. Religious formation has been described as the planned and guided learning experience of religious life with intended learning outcomes.[9] The scarcity of vocations has reduced the number of those in formation programs and has decreased the number of those guiding this experience. While the numbers have declined, formation remains one of the pressing issues of these present times. This quandary includes the education of current and future formation personnel and the initial formation of those entering religious life.[10] *Perfectae Caritatis* clearly states that the suitable renewal of religious communities depends largely on the training and education of their members.[11]

Because of the urgency and necessity of religious formation, the challenges are numerous. The research has elucidated the following critical areas:

1. There is inadequate catechetical formation of a significant number of candidates.

2. There is an increasing age gap between congregational members and those entering religious congregations.

3. There is concern for the preparation of candidates in developing countries.

4. There is a need for a solid theological formation for novices.

5. There are family pressures on candidates not to choose the religious life style.

6. There are problems associated with consumerism in western countries often militating against religious commitment.[12]

The principle purpose of formation at its various stages, initial and ongoing, is to immerse religious in the experience of God and to help them perfect this experience gradually into their lives.[13] How can this purpose be facilitated in the midst of the pressing difficulties and urgent concerns that face religious life today? This is a crucial question which religious need to address as they continue to respond to the challenges of the Second Vatican Council in light of the changing needs of the world at the approach of the Twenty-first Century.

Statement of the Problem

For each religious, formation is a dual process. This double process involves:

1. becoming more fully a disciple of Jesus Christ while increasingly assuming the heart and mind of Christ; and,

2. sharing more deeply in Christ's gift of himself to God while ministering to the human family.

Such a dual process requires a genuine conversion. This conversion reaches not only to spiritual values but also to those which contribute psychologically, culturally, and socially to the fullness of the human personality.[14] The initial formation process and the subsequent commitment to the evangelical counsels does not constitute an obstacle to the true development of the human person but by its very nature is extremely beneficial to that development.[15]

This formation is not achieved all at once. The journey from the first to the final response falls broadly into four phases:

1. the prenovitiate, in which the genuineness of the call is identified as far as possible;

2. the novitiate which is the initiation into a new form of life;

3. first profession and the period of maturing prior to perpetual profession;

4. perpetual profession and the ongoing formation of the mature years.

The stages of novitiate and first profession are especially important because they lead to the incorporation of new members into a congregation. Therefore, they are specifically determined by Church law and detailed in the Constitutions of each religious congregation.[16]

This study is based on two assumptions. The **first assumption** is that the novitiate experience is an essential component of the formation process in religious communities. Religious life begins with the novitiate. Whatever may be the special aim of the institute, the principal purpose of the novitiate is to initiate the novice into the essential requirements of the religious life and to implement the evangelical counsels of chastity, poverty, and obedience. Consequently, in the formation cycle, the novitiate serves an irreplaceable and privileged role as the first introduction into religious life. This period offers time for novices to experience gradual familiarity with the religious way of life and with their own ability to live that life before making a vowed commitment.[17]

The **second assumption** is that learning and behavioral change in the novice is expected to occur by the end of the novitiate experience. The novitiate must be designed explicitly to develop the novice's understanding and living of religious life within a particular congregation. This education is formulated through the systematic construction of knowledge and experience, under the auspices of personnel suited to the task of aiding and evaluating a candidate's continuous growth in personal, social, and spiritual competence. This learning and behavior change is assessed in an environment that facilitates a discernment by the novice and the formation personnel of the novice's ability and willingness to live the religious life. This discernment is critical since formation is the process of becoming more completely a disciple of Jesus Christ and since such a process requires a genuine conversion in the novice which bears fruit spiritually, psychologically, culturally, and socially.[18]

Because of the central place of the novitiate in religious life and the novice's learning that is intended to occur during this time, the necessity of a sound theological foundation for the novitiate could hardly be overstated. Bernard Lonergan has proposed a contemporary method for theology and has located the foundation of this theology in the notion of conversion. Since the formation process necessitates a genuine conversion within the novice, Lonergan's theological method offers a possible framework for such a program.[19]

Lonergan's formulation of conversion through the modes of intellectual, moral, and religious conversion suggests a uniqueness not found in other theologies. This unique differentiation of conversion meets the novice in his or her own singularity. Since each one is distinct and has various and progressive levels of consciousness, much time is required to get to know each level and to surrender that level to God. The three dimensions of conversion assist growth in awareness of these levels of consciousness and in the transformation needed at each level.

The differentiation in conversion takes into account the various aspects of novices and the progressive growth and transformation that are needed at different points in their life. Furthermore, this differentiation in conversion meets them where they are along life's journey and offers them the opportunities and life experiences needed to continue to transcend themselves in their experiencing, understanding, judging, deciding, and loving.

This necessity of a theological foundation for the novitiate necessitates an exploratory study of the behaviors expected of the novice upon the completion of the novitiate. Such an analysis would address the following points:

1. the centrality of the novitiate in religious life; and,

2. the learning and behavior change expected in the novice during this time period.

As a result of this study, appropriate learning experiences could then be incorporated into the novitiate to facilitate the attainment of these behaviors. This study would assist congregations to plan appropriately and to implement their novitiate programs based on a theological foundation. Such an investigation would demonstrate the importance of a theological foundation and would examine what behaviors are considered important for a novice to manifest at the completion of the novitiate.

Statement of Purpose

The purpose of this study was to explore the necessity of a theological foundation for the novitiate experience in light of the behaviors expected of a novice by the novice director upon the completion of the novitiate.

Utilizing a questionnaire, Katie described behaviors using the Lonergonian dimensions of moral, intellectual, and religious conversion to determine the degree of importance the novice director gave to each dimension of conversion. The study also determined if there was a relationship between the category of conversion which was identified and the type of congregation of the novice director.

The research specifically focused on the expectations of the novice by the novice director during the academic year 1987-1988 and included women and men novice directors who attended the National Congress of the Religious Formation Conference in October, 1987.

Katie's study addressed the following research questions:

1. Is there a significant difference among the dimensions of conversion (moral, intellectual, and religious) emphasized in novitiate programs?

2. Is there a significant difference among apostolic, monastic, and evangelical congregations relative to the dimension of conversion identified in their novitiate programs?

3. What is the most important concept or behavior for a novice to learn and integrate into her or his own life by the end of the novitiate?

Definition of Terms

The terms specific to this study were: moral conversion, intellectual conversion, religious conversion, apostolic congregation, monastic congregation, and evangelical congregation.

Moral conversion changes the criterion of a person's decision and choices from satisfaction to values. . . . Moral conversion consists in personally opting for the truly good, for value in place of satisfaction when value and satisfaction conflict.[20]

Intellectual conversion is a radical clarification of knowing and the elimination of the myth that reality is what is seen. Knowing is not just seeing; it is experiencing, understanding, judging, and believing. Reality is not just looked at; reality is given in experience, organized and extrapolated by understanding and affirmed by judgment and belief. Intellectual conversion is the realization that the world is mediated by meaning, that the world is not known by the person's sense experience but by the external and internal experience of a community, and by the continuously checked and rechecked judgments of that community.[21]

Religious conversion is God's love flooding the person's heart through the Holy Spirit. Religious conversion is a total and permanent self-surrender to God without conditions, qualifications, and reservations. This conversion is characterized by an increasing simplicity and passivity in prayer.[22]

An *apostolic congregation* is defined as one in which the ministry of the group is the primary determining influence in the daily life of the members. The focus of the group is mobility and apostolic availability. The unity in mind and heart of the members goes beyond physical presence.[23]

A *monastic congregation* is defined as one in which formal prayer is the primary determining influence in the daily life of the members. The focus of the group is stability, solitude, and peace. Physical presence is important to maintain the unity in mind and heart of the members.[24]

An *evangelical congregation* is defined as one in which community and fellowship are the primary determining influences in the daily life of the members. The focus of the group is community directed toward the person. The primary ministry is service through sisterhood and brotherhood. This ministry focuses on being with and among people in simplicity and benevolence.[25]

Limitations of the Study

One limitation was that there were some novice directors who did not attend the conference. Consequently, their responses on this topic could not be a part of the study.

A second limitation was that some of the statements are so necessary to spiritual development that it might have been difficult for the directors to rate them in the area of "little importance."

A third limitation was related to the 72% response rate. Those directors at the conference who chose not to respond may have had different perceptions than those who did respond to the questionnaire.

Finally, Katie inevitably brought to this study a personal bias since she was a novice director herself for six years and had her own thoughts and feelings concerning the novitiate process. However, in contrast to this limitation, her knowledge, experience, and understanding of religious formation was a valuable asset in the development and implementation of the study.

Notes

1. Walter M. Abbott, ed., *The Documents of Vatican II. Perfectae Caritatis: Decree on the Appropriate Renewal of the Religious Life.* (London: Geoffrey Chapman, 1967) #2.

2. John Carroll Futrell, "The Future of Religious Life," *Human Development* 2 (1981):7.

3. Archbishop John Quinn, "Extending the Dialogue about Religious Life," *Origins* 13 (1983): 215-216.

4. Futrell, 7.

5. Union of Superiors General, "Representatives of Men's Orders Meet with the Pope," *Origins* 13 (1983): 487.

6. Futrell, 8.

7. Patrick Granfield, "Changes in Religious Life: Freedom, Responsibility, Community," *America* 151 (1984): 121.

8. Union of Superiors General, 487. Quinn, 215-216.

9. Martin O'Reilly, "Current Conceptions of Religious Formation: An Analysis," *Review for Religious* 44 (1985): 807.

10. Union of Superiors General, 488.

11. *Perfectae Caritatis*, #18.

12. International Union of Superiors General, "Women Religious Meet with Pope to Discuss their Life," *Origins* 13 (1983): 483.

13. Vatican Congregation for Religious and for Secular Institutes, "Contemplative Dimension of Religious Life," *Origins* 10 (1980): #17.

14. Vatican Congregation for Religious and for Secular Institutes, "Essential Elements in Church Teaching on Religious Life," *Origins* 13 (1983): #45.

15. Abbott, *Lumen Gentium: Dogmatic Constitution on the Church*, #46.

16. "Essential Elements," #48.

17. "Essential Elements," # 48. Vatican Congregation for Religious and for Secular Institutes, "Renovationis Causam: Instruction on the Renewal of Formation for Religious Life," *The Way Supplement* 7 (1969): #13. "Renovationis Causam," #4. Jean Steffes, "A Model for Individual Formation of Apostolic Religious Women," *Review for Religious* 39 (1980): 678.

18. Joel Giallanza and John Gleason, "Reflection on Initial Formation," *Human Development* 5 (1984): 15-20. "Essential Elements," #45. O'Reilly, 807.

19. Bernard Lonergan, *Method in Theology* (Minneapolis: Winston, 1972). Miriam Gramlich, "Ongoing Conversion and Religious Life," *Review for Religious* 40 (1981): 819.

20. Lonergan, *Method* 240.

21. Lonergan, *Method* 238.

22. Lonergan, *Method* 240-241.

23. George Aschenbrenner, "Apostolic Spirituality." Workshop on Apostolic Spirituality, New Orleans, LA. 1980.

24. Aschenbrenner, 1980.

25. Taken from the *TOR Commentary* and the writings of four Franciscans: Joe Chinnici, Jean Francois Godet, Peter Van Leeuwen, and William Short.

Chapter Two

Review of the Literature

During the initial part of Katie's search, she described the problem, discussed the assumptions, stated her purpose, defined the terms, and listed the limitations. The next part of her flight took her through a review of the literature pertinent to this topic which included:

1. the differences in monastic, apostolic, and evangelical congregations;

2. the characteristics of novitiate formation in religious congregations;

3. some models for novitiate formation; and

4. an examination of Bernard Lonergan's theology of conversion as a foundation for the novitiate experience.

The call to discipleship has always been at the core of Christianity.[1] From early days of Christianity, diverse modes of life emerged to express the essentials of discipleship. Religious life came into existence as one of the ways to follow the teachings of Jesus Christ. Throughout history this life has evolved in various forms in response to the needs, movements, and culture of the time.[2] A key moment in that evolution in the Twentieth Century was the action of the Second Vatican Council.

This Council took upon itself the task of renewal of the Catholic Church. This renewal was done in order that the Church might experience an increase of spiritual power and be better equipped to communicate the gospel message to the modern world. The Council gave serious consideration to those called by God to religious life and mandated that religious communities return to their founding charism.[3] The Decree, *Perfectae Caritatis*, also introduced a significant distinction between monastic and apostolic congregations.[4]

Types of Congregations

In the monastic lifestyle, the formal prayer of the congregation, Liturgy of the Hours and the Eucharist, has a clear and decisive primacy in the development of the whole way of life. These times of formal prayer are the first items placed in the daily schedule. They literally determine the schedule and the contour of the daily life of the members and are the primary apostolate or ministry of the monastic religious. Because of the clear priority of the Liturgy of the Hours and the Eucharist, the monastic life is characterized by a regularity of order and schedule. Often, only special feast days will vary the routine of the monastic life.[5]

This monastic spirit requires an appropriate withdrawal from the world and is expressed in many different ways. Some monasteries are situated in secluded areas; others are located in the midst of an inner city. Sometimes the separation is a small, simple apartment-hermitage. This isolation from the world is not an end in itself, nor an uncaring protection from the world. For the monastic religious, it is precisely through being set apart from the world that a care and concern for the world grows and is appropriately expressed.[6]

The monastic congregation is united in a special way through vowed stability. This stability unifies religious in a specific place with a communal bond that facilitates their ongoing search together for a deeper union with God. This kind of external stability stimulates a profound communal experience of God in the monastic life. A physical togetherness in prayer, work, reading, eating, and recreating are further aspects of this monastic dynamic.[7]

The characteristics of apostolic congregations present a different picture. When describing the apostolic dynamic in terms of religious life, the Vatican Council speaks of congregations in which "the very nature of the religious life requires apostolic action and services."[8] All forms of religious life do imply apostolic love, and frequently also some form of apostolic activity. However, in the apostolic form of religious life there is an intrinsic union and a profound reciprocity between the interior life and the apostolic life. This intrinsic union enables the apostolic religious to lead one life, not a double life. Consequently, this is a vocation in which spirit and activity, prayer and apostolate, common life and common action come together in a balanced whole.[9]

For the apostolic religious, ministerial involvement determines the contour and the schedule of daily life rather than formal prayer. While not denying the importance of regular prayer, the point to be stressed here concerns the influence that ministry has on the whole makeup of the active life. The legitimate demands of ministry form the schedule of the day. These religious must first insert themselves into ministry and ascertain an honest sense of its reasonable demands. Only then can their conviction about regular contemplation determine the specifics of when, where, and how long they should pray each day. Regardless of ministry, the necessity of regular contemplation is beyond doubt. But the determination of the specifics of regular contemplation depends upon the demands of the ministry.[10]

Because busy ministry and service of others are essential to active spirituality, a regular routine scheduled around formal prayer is not possible. A flexibility of heart and spirit is needed in order to respond to the challenges and needs of a changing world. While a certain routine is necessary for all human life, the active apostle must always resist the escape into an overly monastic routine and must learn to trust the gift of flexibility that is always part of the active dynamic in the Church.[11]

The typical and more important prayer of the active apostle is a distinctively prayerful presence in and through all activity. This prayerful presence is related to the necessity to find, to be with, and to serve God in all action. The prayer of the apostolate involves two mutual and integral movements. The first is an appropriate, regular involvement in contemplation, which gradually spills over and renders prayerful everything the active apostle does, says, and is. The second is an involvement in activity which stirs a desire for, and sometimes provides the subject matter of contemplative prayer. As one grows faithful and sensitive to these two movements, a prayerful presence in all activity develops and grows.[12]

Thus prayer and action are not completely separate moments. Prayer pervades action, yet the primary action of apostles is their prayer and love for God and the people of God. As prayer is transformed by a physical act into a liturgical gesture or a spoken word, so the interior life of apostolic religious finds expression in apostolic ministry. These integral and fluid movements enable apostolic religious to be contemplative in their apostolate and apostolic in their contemplation.[13]

The apostolic congregation would be deficient in its unified faith vision if each member did not share the same desire to pray together regularly. This desire needs to take expression in physical presence whenever ministry permits. The active charism does not depend as much on the physical presence of the members to each other as the monastic charism but a specific union is required if the active charism is to be life-giving to the members. This unity must be rooted deeply in the hearts of all the members and must be manifested in a willingness to come and share time together in prayer and recreating activities whenever ministry makes this possible.[14]

In differentiating apostolic life and the evangelical life, Jean Godet explains that the apostolic life is the life of the early Church under the apostles. Jesus had returned to the Father and the apostles were sent (apostolos) on mission.[15] They had tasks to perform. They were to preach the gospel, announce the Lord's resurrection, establish and organize local communities of Christians, and found the Church.[16]

The evangelical life has a different model which is not that of the first apostles in the Acts working for the above tasks. The model here is the life of the disciples with Jesus. Jesus lives with them and teaches them along the way. The disciples try to learn by looking at and listening to him. The evangelical life attempts to understand the disciple's life with Christ and to do the same thing.[17] Jesus' life in the gospels becomes the model; the gospels become the point of reference. The task is good example, living the gospel in simplicity and joy.[18]

In the evangelical life there is no distinction between contemplation and action; evangelicals do both. They contemplate and look at Jesus; they act by performing and acting as Jesus did. In the evangelical life, the question is NOT: what are you *doing*? Since, they are concerned about acting as Jesus did and in "doing nothing specific," the emphasis is on *being*. Because of this accent, they are not usually in charge of organizing or changing systems.[19]

The evangelical life is living in contemplation and action together at the same time. Evangelicals must live in the presence of God, looking and listening to Jesus in an ongoing way. In daily life no-thing is particular and yet each thing is special. Evangelicals are called to live according to the gospel as brothers and sisters. St. Francis of Assisi understood that all are God's children, all are brothers and sisters. To make this real and concrete, it is important that evangelicals come with nothing. For the school of Jesus, nothing is needed; no tuition is required. Since each member has nothing, each person is equal; each is light and free.[20]

The way evangelical religious relate with people is important. Their purpose is to live and establish relationships with others. Thus evangelicals work as servants in order to build fellowship. These relationships mean peace for building the Kingdom of God. If evangelicals wish to build relationships as the center of their lives, they must not be possessed or possess anything that is an obstacle between the neighbor and themselves.[21]

To differentiate further the apostolic and evangelical congregations, the apostolic life focuses on ministry first. The members must organize their lives to accomplish the ministry. In the evangelical life, there is no specific task but to live the gospel. Their primary ministry is sisterhood and brotherhood. The accent is on the familial qualities of trust and reverence for one another. Organization is not needed to accomplish the proclamation of the good news in the evangelical life.[22]

Another difference between the apostolic and evangelical lifestyles is that apostolic religious primarily work for and within the Church. In the evangelical life, the focus is more outside the Church than inside. This shift for the evangelical lifestyle is congruent with Jesus' thrust of sending the disciples out to all the nations as the focus for mission.[23]

To summarize the characteristics of these three types of congregations, their distinguishing features can be described as follows:

1. The monastic congregation is centered on contemplation and the praise of God; their model is the hidden life of Jesus in Nazareth before his public life and the hermits of the desert of the Fourth Century.

2. The apostolic congregation is centered on the concrete mission of service to the world, with the members in common solidarity for this mission; their model is the life of the disciples after Jesus' Ascension.

3. The evangelical congregation is centered on relationships in a spirit of simplicity and benevolence, and on a radical witness to Christ and his gospel; their model is the disciples with Jesus during his earthly life.[24]

Religious Formation

The Second Vatican Council also addressed the significance and future of religious life in *Perfectae Caritatis*. The document stated that an integral part of that future is the women and men who are today embracing the religious life.[25] The Council clearly stated that the renewal and future of each religious congregation depends most of all on the initial formation of new members.[26]

This formation is essentially a process of gradual preparation for the total and perpetual offering of the person to Jesus Christ through the profession of the vows of poverty, celibacy, and obedience in the Church.[27] Religious profession is conceived as a loving response to the invitation of Christ, who calls the religious to follow him and to share his life and mission. In essence, religious life is an intimate and personal relationship with the person of Christ.[28] Therefore, the best formation and preparation for religious profession must be given to the candidates.

This initial formation includes both the time of the novitiate and the years following first vows. However, the novitiate is of primary importance because it is intimately concerned with the very beginnings of religious life.[29] Technically, religious life begins with the novitiate. The purpose of the novitiate is to initiate the person into religious life as the novice learns the primary essentials of the life and begins to live out the evangelical counsels of poverty, celibacy, and obedience.[30]

Admittance to the novitiate ought to be based on sound criteria. Novices should be admitted to the novitiate when they are conscious of having been called by God. This awareness of vocation is accompanied by a compelling and overriding need to seek out the person of Christ, to learn more about him and to draw closer to him. Every kind of authentic love manifests this same need to be **with** the beloved. The novice should enter into the novitiate in response to an interior need and a conscious search to hear the voice of Jesus Christ and to learn from him. This search will draw the novice more closely to Christ and will develop the familiarity with Christ which is the essential mark of the true religious who leaves all things to follow Christ.[31]

Novices should be admitted to the novitiate when they have achieved some degree of human and spiritual maturity which will enable them to respond to this vocation with sufficient knowledge, personal responsibility, and free will. These elements of sufficient knowledge, personal responsibility and free will place novices on the cutting edge of their own formation. This implies that the novices have the primary duty for their own formation and are ultimately responsible for saying "yes" or "no" to the call to religious life. No one can take the novices' place in giving a response that must be offered in freedom and love. But this also connotes that novices must become aware in a very personal and mature way of what is expected of them in a vowed relationship with the Lord.[32]

The novitiate should provide the kind of environment that is conducive to the continued development of the Christian personality so that novices will continue their spiritual and human development. This ongoing maturity should be characterized by a growing self knowledge and an ability to act responsibly and to make appropriate choices. This continued development is essential for novices to be grounded in their personal identity, so they can deal with the demands of assuming a congregational identity. Consequently, experiences which foster personal identity and congregational identity are essential.[33]

The novitiate must also emphasize the study and meditation of sacred scripture as well as instruction in the theory and practice of spirituality. This emphasis is vital for the development of a spiritual life and for an interior grasp of the religious state. The novice should also be introduced to the liturgical life of the Church and to the congregation's own special spirit.[34] However, Paul Molinari stresses that the fundamental formative movement of the novitiate is "to facilitate the growing attachment to the person of Christ and to his manner of life. Whatever else is offered should complement this aim."[35]

The director who is to facilitate the novitiate process must have a knowledge of sacred scripture, theology, and human nature. In addition, the director should have an understanding of psychology, sociology, anthropology, and human biology. However, what is wanted and needed most in a director is wisdom. This implies knowledge which has been assimilated and seasoned, not just knowledge which has been acquired.[36] The Sacred Congregation for Religious and Secular Institutes has explicitly spoken about the need for qualified formation personnel. The Congregation has stated that those responsible for formation need to possess:

1. the human qualities of insight and responsiveness;

2. a certain experiential knowledge of God and of prayer;

3. wisdom resulting from attentive and prolonged listening to the word of God;

4. a love of the sacramental life of the Church and an understanding of its role in spiritual formation;

5. a necessary cultural competence; and

6. sufficient time and goodwill to attend to the candidates individually and not just as a group.[37]

The selection of the right formation personnel is most important because directors must serve as a model for the novices. Directors are needed who can give novices a living inspiration, who can communicate to the novices that religious life is worth embracing. Additionally, directors need to be people of vision and imagination, alive to new developments and opportunities in the Church and society. They need to possess an inner coherence, strength, and conviction.[38]

The directors' conviction must be manifested in a readiness to relate and to communicate, in a willingness to accept and to hear questions of all kinds from various community segments while remaining free and committed to their role and to the novices in their care.[39] Consequently, it is vital that while attending to the spiritual and emotional maturing process of the novices, directors insure their own integrity by continuing their own growth and development.

For those who possess an intimate knowledge of God's ways and of the principles of spiritual direction, the necessity of a systematic inception into religious life is evident. This introduction demands an extended time period for recollection and prayer, study, and reflection. In fact, when one takes into account the meaning and demands of the novitiate, the importance of a reasonable length of time for this formation interval is indubitable.[40]

Church law states that the novitiate must last for twelve months to be valid, but should not last longer than two years.[41] The goal of this restriction is to guard against placing novices in an extended period of indecision. After two years of study, prayer, reflection, and experience in the congregation, the novice and formation personnel need to decide if the novice is able to make a vowed commitment in this particular congregation.

To facilitate the decision of the novice and formation personnel, various models of the novitiate have been discussed in the literature. A few of these models presented in current articles include the therapeutic model, prophetic model, ecclesial model, decisional model, initiative model. Traditional topics such as prayer, the vows, ministry, the history and spirit of the congregation can be included in any of the models. As with all models, these need not be mutually exclusive and no one of these models exhausts the reality of formation.

The therapeutic model is oriented towards psychology and stresses the growth of the individual through techniques such as counseling, journal keeping, active imagination, dream analysis, and other methods borrowed from psychology. The prophetic model is oriented towards social justice and stresses social analysis, direct experiences with poor and marginalized persons, and the need to confront unjust political, economic, and ecclesial structures. The ecclesial model is oriented towards the sacramental life of the Church. This model stresses the interaction between the person in formation and the congregation which the novice is joining and the ritualizing of the steps in the formation process.[42]

The decisional model is employed by groups admitting candidates who have successfully addressed most of the ordinary growth issues of later adolescence. These candidates have come to a healthy integration of their roles as young adults and Church members. They now seek to define a lifestyle that expresses a life-time commitment to the Lord. The novitiate is one of the final steps in this decision or discernment process. According to this model, a person comes to the novitiate with experience in prayer, with a good background in theology and scriptural studies, with ego strengths necessary for attaining and sustaining an authentic sense of identity, and with the desire to serve the Lord. During the novitiate of decision, novices experience an environment conducive to serious reflection, advanced direction in the spiritual life, and an intense spiritual journey that leads to making a final commitment to God in a certain congregation.[43]

The initiative model is employed by groups accepting candidates earlier in the discernment process usually after a probationary period.[44] This probationary period allows the formation personnel and candidates the opportunity to determine whether or not candidates are "endowed with such elements of human and emotional maturity as will afford grounds for hope that they are capable of undertaking properly the obligations of the religious state; and that in the religious life and especially in the novitiate, they will be able to progress toward fuller maturity."[45]

Whether or not one model or a combination of models is chosen for the novitiate, a sound theological foundation is requisite for the experience.[46] Bernard Lonergan describes theology as a reflection on religion.[47] Theology, as a reflection on religion, is needed to decide precisely the aims, purposes, and assumptions of the religious experience. If this reflection is not done, the experience may fall prey to the whims and fantasies of a particular director, administration, or community group. Consequently, a theological foundation is also necessary for the novitiate experience to determine the aims, purposes, assumptions, and the ground of this experience in religious life. A theological foundation will root the novitiate experience in a particular raison d'etre and will prevent the novitiate from being captured by any person or group and being turned in all directions.[48]

Conversion

Lonergan has proposed a contemporary method for theology and has situated this theology in conversion.[49] Lonergan's theological method in which the notion of conversion plays a central role offers a foundation for the novitiate experience since the novitiate necessitates a genuine conversion within the novice.[50] Lonergan defines conversion as a fateful call to a dreaded holiness, as an about-face by which we move into a radically new horizon, as a personal entrance of God into our life and history, as a communication of God to us.[51] Through this experience, we are transformed; our world is transformed.

Normally conversion is a prolonged process although the explicit acknowledgment may be concentrated in a few momentous judgments and decisions.[52] In addition, conversion is not just a development or even a series of developments, but a resultant change of course and direction. We experience our eyes being opened and our former world fading and falling away. Something new emerges that causes developments on all levels and in all areas of our human living.[53] Conversion is never the logical consequence of a previous position. On the contrary, it is a radical revision of that position which transforms us and makes us capable of grasping not merely conclusions but principles as well.[54] The former principles determining our life are now radically changed and like the merchant searching for fine pearls when the one gem of singular magnificence is discovered and we bask in its glow, everything else can be relinquished (Matt. 13:45-46).

Consequently, more than a direct continuation or expansion of a previous horizontal development, conversion is a vertical move which "begins a new sequence that can keep revealing ever greater depth and breadth and wealth."[55] Conversion affects all of our conscious and intentional operations. Conversion directs the gaze, pervades the imagination, releases the symbols that penetrate to the depth of the psyche, enriches the understanding, guides the judgments, and reinforces the decisions of the converted.[56]

This vertical direction causes us to move from one set of roots to another and this occurs only inasmuch as we discover what is unauthentic in ourselves and we turn away from this unauthenticity. This turning away enables us to discover what the fullness of human authenticity can be and to embrace this authenticity with our whole being.[57] The gospel message of Mark (1:15) is echoed in this turning away from unauthenticity: "Repent and reform your lives! The Kingdom of God is at hand!"

The task of repentance and conversion is a life-long process. We are restless creatures with a never-ending drive for self transcendence which impels us to go beyond self and ultimately to encounter the God who alone can satisfy every longing. But that drive is not a random or haphazard experience. Rather, the drive follows a discernible pattern which reflects the basic structure of our human spirits. Lonergan identifies the basic pattern of human operations as:

imagining,
experiencing,
understanding,
judging,
deciding,
believing,
acting, and
loving.

By recognizing and respecting these basic patterns, we can better assist and facilitate our journey to God.[58]

Although conversion is intensely personal and utterly intimate, it is not so private as to be solitary. Conversion can happen to many, and they can form a community. The community functions to sustain the members in their self-transformation and to help them in working out the implications and fulfilling the promise of their new life. Finally, what has become communal can become historical. The communal conversion can pass from generation to generation, from one cultural milieu to another. The communal conversion can adapt to changing circumstances, confront new situations, survive into a different age, flourish into another period.[59] Thus an intensely personal experience has the potential to become a communal phenomenon and an historical event. This has been evidenced in the lives of such people as Francis of Assisi, Ignatius of Loyola, Theresa of Avila, Dorothy Day, Bishop Oscar Romero.

What happens when the conversion process is missing within a person, a community, a generation? The absence of conversion is manifested by sinfulness and selfishness. There is a sustained superficiality that evades questions; uncomfortable and disturbing queries are avoided. There is an inordinate attachment to all that the world offers to distract the mind and relax the body. There is a personal absorption in the fulfillment of personal needs to the detriment or neglect of others. However, this escape into individual comfortability is not without a price. The deficiency of conversion reveals itself in unrest, in the absence of joy in the pursuit of fun, in the lack of inner peace.[60]

When conversion is present, Lonergan sees this process at work on a number of levels and describes several different conversions which a person may experience: intellectual conversion, moral conversion, and religious conversion. In order of exposition Lonergan prefers to explain first intellectual, then moral, and lastly religious conversion. But he admits that the three conversions generally occur in the reverse direction. We first respond to God's offer of love, and then we are led to moral and intellectual conversion. What is common to conversion on all these levels is the decision to turn away from what is unauthentic in life, to awaken to new meaning, and to commit to a distinct way of living in the world.[61]

Intellectual Conversion

In discussing the three modes of conversion, Katie used Lonergan's preferential explanatory mode and began with intellectual conversion.

Intellectual conversion underscores the critical role of human knowledge and reflection in our lives. Human knowing is a dynamic structure in the sense that a whole has parts and the whole is related to each of the parts. Also each of the parts is related to one another and to the whole.[62] Human knowing involves many distinct activities:

seeing, hearing, smelling, touching, tasting, inquiring, imagining, understanding, conceiving, reflecting, weighing the evidence, and judging.

No one of these activities alone, for example — seeing or hearing or tasting — may be named human knowing. What is true of sense, is also true of understanding. Without the prior experiences of the senses, there is nothing for us to understand. Moreover, the combination of the operations of sense and of understanding does not suffice for human knowing. There must be added judging. Nor can we emphasize judging in human knowing to the exclusion of experience and understanding. Hence, human knowing is a whole whose parts are operations forming a dynamic structure.[63]

Lonergan explicates several levels in this structure of knowing and designates these levels as follows:

1. experiencing;

2. understanding;

3. judging; and,

4. deciding.

On the experiential or empirical level, we sense, perceive, imagine, feel, speak, and move. On the intellectual level, we inquire, come to understand, express what we have understood, and work out the presuppositions and implications of the expression. On the rational level, we reflect, marshal the evidence, and pass judgment on the truth or falsity, certainty or probability of a statement. On the decisional level, we deliberate about possible courses of action, decide, and carry out the decision.[64]

In addition, there are distinct differences among the levels of experiencing, understanding, judging, and deciding. **Understanding** distinguishes, names, groups, and correlates experiences. Understanding also grasps the precise relations among different sets of experiences and moves to insight. Understanding progresses to insight by first distinguishing and naming experiences and then by becoming aware of the order that keeps one set of data in a specific relationship to another set.[65]

This act of understanding is a real event; there is a distinct change in understanding. This insight is an Eureka experience which is communicated not by a description of data but by an explanation of how the data hang together.[66]   For example, just looking at a plant and seeing its leaves are drooping does not indicate a dry plant.   Some plants droop when they need water and other droop when they are saturated with moisture.   Realizing what the plant is trying to communicate when it has a wilted appearance is an insight into its nature.   A description of data would be the drooping leaves.   Knowing what this data indicates is an explanation of how the information hangs together; this is an Eureka experience!

Judgment returns to the experience to test explanations. We reach reality when we pass judgment on the correctness of our insight.   Only when we check the data again to see whether our understanding leaves no relevant data unexplained can we say whether or not we correctly understand the reality in question.[67]

One of the most startling features about making judgments, and one of the most important, is the criterion used.   The criterion for judgment is the **absence** of relevant questions. We become more firm in our certitude to the degree that we are either ignorant of further questions and conditions, or are convinced that relevant questions could not arise.[68]   An example of this criterion would be the discernment process a novice moves through in making a decision about vows.   When the novice and director have examined all the known questions and issues surrounding the commitment, and have prayerfully reflected on these issues, then a valid judgment based on sound criterion can be made.   To differentiate judgment and understanding, understanding yields explanations.   Judgment, in contrast, yields no explanation; it merely affirms or denies the explanation.   Understanding and judgment are linked inasmuch as the explanations issuing from understanding are still subject to verification.   **Understanding** answers **how or why**; **judgment** answers **whether**.[69]

To move this differentiation a step forward, experience is associated with being attentive; understanding is associated with being intelligent; and judgment is associated with being reasonable and realistic.   Experience corresponds to data;

understanding corresponds to intelligibility; judgment corresponds to reality. Intelligence takes us beyond experience to ask why, how, and what for. Reasonableness takes us beyond the answers of intelligence to ask whether the answers are true and accurate. Responsibility goes beyond fact, desire, and possibility to discern between what is truly good and what is only apparently good. Thus experience, understanding, and judgment have different objects: experience is related to data, understanding to intelligibility, and judgment to reality.[70]

Experience, understanding, and judgment also feel different. When we are merely attentive, we are observant, sensitive, and experiencing. We are not asking questions about what we are experiencing. When we do ask a question about what we experience, we wonder why or how. We play with the data and maybe enjoy an insight that gives a plausible explanation. So the feeling of being intelligent is quite different from the feeling of being attentive. When we move to the judgment that settles on which explanation best fits the experience, consciousness changes and the feeling aroused is one of being reasonable and realistic.[71]

The experience of human knowing is also qualitatively differentiated. When we are seeing or hearing, touching or tasting, we are experiencing our own sensitivity. When we are inquiring, understanding, conceiving, thinking, we are experiencing our own intelligence. When we are reflecting, weighing the evidence, judging, we are experiencing our own rationality. Just as intelligence is quite different from sensitivity, so the experience of intelligence is quite different from the experience of sensitivity. Just as rationality is quite different from intelligence, so the experience of rationality is quite different from the experience of intelligence.[72]

Consequently, human knowing is self-assembling and self-constituting. Human knowing puts itself together, one part summoning forth the next, till the whole is reached. Experience stimulates inquiry, and inquiry is intelligence bringing itself to act. Human knowing leads from experience through imagination to insight, and from insight to the concepts that combine in single objects both what has been grasped by insight and what in experience is relevant to the insight. In turn, concepts stimulate reflection, and reflection requires rationality. Reason marshals the evidence and weighs it either to judge or else to doubt and so renew inquiry.[73] To envision how each of these parts flow into the next, we can imagine a squiggly propelling itself forward down the steps. Each ring of the squiggly is connected and the action of one ring moves the others forward in a continual motion as the movement of one ring summons forth the movement of the next ring.

Another element in human knowing is belief because while knowing is a compound of experience, understanding, judgment, and deciding very little of what is known has come from personal experience, understanding, and judgment. Much knowledge comes from believing others through family stories, television, and printed material. And yet, what is believed has originated in the verified understanding of some other person because when we believe others we are depending upon their experience, understanding, and judgment. Even when we are skeptical, we are not skeptical about the value of belief in general. On the contrary, we are anxious to eliminate mistakes from our set of beliefs, because without belief we would know practically nothing.[74]

The knowledge that comes to us through belief does not necessarily begin from the immanently generated knowledge of one person. For example, there is a fair degree of certainty that wearing seat belts helps to prevent traffic fatalities. This conclusion has been reached through individuals escaping or suffering injury; statisticians reporting data; researchers examining data; theoreticians pursuing insight into data; and a conclusion being reached. This knowledge was generated by the direct experience of a large group, a combination of beliefs and insights by a smaller group, and a judgment reached by a few, which they present for the belief of a larger group so that traffic fatalities may be decreased or avoided.[75]

Thus an act of belief involves a judgment of value which concerns the worth of something that already exists or the worth of bringing something into existence. Essentially, the act of belief includes three discernible value judgments.[76]

First, there is the general judgment that it is better to believe other people than to start from a Cartesian universal skepticism.

Secondly, there is deliberation on the trustworthiness of sources.

Thirdly, there is deliberation on the value of believing specific content.

Judgments of value relative to believing specific content move us from the cognitive sphere to the moral sphere. This sphere of value judgments will be discussed in detail in the section on moral conversion but this is already some glimpse as to how intellectual and moral conversion will eventually be intertwined. However, belief remains an extremely important part of human knowing.[77] For example, think of the terminally ill, who normally go through a period of disbelief and denial that their death is immanent; or ponder the disbelief of the Western world surrounding the possibility of the Jewish holocaust during World War II. Belief does not involve the incidental pieces of knowledge that give us a view of nature and history; rather, belief involves the awesome possibilities for malice or glory, for life or death within the human reach. Consequently, the most significant realities that can be known are constituted by attention, intelligence, reason, decision, and belief.[78]

Each of the different activities is a partial element in the synthesis of human knowing and each element sublates the next element. Sublation means that each element goes beyond the previous one, but brings the previous element forward. That is, each element goes beyond the prior one in an additive fashion. When added, all the elements unite to form the dynamic structure of human knowing.[79] Lonergan delineates the following dimensions of human knowledge and names these dimensions transcendental precepts:

1. be attentive — advert to our own attending;

2. be intelligent—advert to our own intelligence;

3. be reasonable—advert to our own reasonableness; and

4. be responsible—advert to our own deliberations.[80]

First, to be attentive means that we pay careful attention to those things which give delight, which promise pleasure, which threaten danger. Secondly, to be intelligent means that we pay attention to our own intelligence. We are aware when our intelligence fails to understand or when our intelligence is dissatisfied with explanations that do not quite explain. We are also aware of our intellectual search for further questions, of its joy when a solution comes to light, and of its care to find the exact expression to convey precisely what understanding has grasped. Thirdly, to be reasonable reveals a basic type of normativeness—ideas are fine, but they are not enough. The practical person wants to know whether ideas will work. The theoretical person wonders whether ideas are true. Their reasonableness demands sufficient evidence, gathers and weighs all the evidence present, assents when evidence is sufficient and may not assent when evidence is insufficient. Finally, to be responsible means because we are free, we are also responsible. Just as we cannot be reasonable and pass judgment beyond or against the evidence, so too if we are to be obedient to the transcendental precepts, we cannot be responsible without adverting to what is right and wrong in our choices and deliberations. All these dimensions comprise human knowledge and lead us to intellectual conversion through inner conviction and objective truth. Thus inner conviction and objective truth are the fruits of being attentive, intelligent, reasonable, and responsible.[81]

Through this dynamic structure, Lonergan rejects the belief that knowing is a simple, homogeneous act whose finest paradigm is intuition or looking or perceiving. In fact, one of the purposes of his book, *Insight*, is to show the malignant effects of the assumption that a theoretical account of knowing is best modeled on intellectual intuition. Lonergan explains that intellectual conversion is a radical clarification of an exceedingly misleading myth concerning reality, objectivity, and human knowledge. This myth says that knowing is like looking, that objectivity is seeing what is there to be seen and not seeing what is not there. It holds that the real is what is out there now to be visualized. This illusion overlooks the distinction between the world of immediacy and the world mediated by meaning. The world of immediacy is the world of the infant and includes the sum of what is seen, heard, touched, tasted, smelled, and felt. This childish world conforms well to the myth's view of reality, objectivity, and knowledge. Lonergan insists that this world is but a tiny fragment of the world mediated by meaning.[82]

Consequently, the world mediated by meaning is not just seen but also includes what is experienced, understood, reasoned, judged, and believed. In this world, the standard of objectivity is not just the norm of ocular vision. Rather, the norm is the compounded criteria of experiencing, understanding, reasoning, judging, and believing. The reality known is not just visualized, but is given in experience, organized and extrapolated by understanding, weighed by reasoning, affirmed by judgment and belief.[83]

The problem with this myth of the world of immediacy is the assumption that all knowing is something like looking. For us to be liberated from this myth and to discover the self-transcendence proper to the human process of coming to know, we have to break long-ingrained habits of thought and speech. We have to acquire the mastery in our own intellect that is to be had only when we realize precisely what we are doing through the event of human knowing. This realization of self as a knower is intellectual conversion and is a new beginning, a fresh start. Intellectual conversion enables us to grasp that our knowing is a set of functionally interrelated elements of being attentive, intelligent, reasonable, and responsible.

> Be attentive—respect all data as possibly intelligible.
> Be intelligent—correlate our experiences.
> Be reasonable—test the explanations.
> Be responsible—accept responsibility for our decisions.

In essence, be obedient to the transcendental precepts.[84]

Intellectual conversion consists essentially in discovering and taking possession of our own questioning and cognitive operations as dynamically structured and oriented toward self-transcendence. We can reflect on and verify not only the existence of our own experiencing, understanding, and judging, but also the structured dynamism of these cognitive operations. In other words, we can attend to our experiencing, understanding, reasoning, and deciding. We can understand the unity, the relations, and the immanent norms of experiencing, understanding, reasoning, and deciding. We can also affirm the reality of our experienced and understood experiencing, understanding, reasoning, and deciding. We assert, concretely, that we do perform these operations as experienced and understood, that we are in this sense, knowers. We utilize the dynamics of human knowing.[85]

The appropriation of intellectual conversion is not something that happens in its fullness all at once. Occasionally we observe distinct facets of this personal process being manifested. We need to discover and take possession of the intelligence which actually belongs to us. We need to appropriate our own mind and thereby transform life through this creative power.[86]

Central to the possession we take of ourselves as knowers in intellectual conversion is the specific realization that the criterion of the real is the "virtually unconditioned" of our own judgment and decision. This insight is the basis for the elimination of the myth about reality and objectivity as well as of human knowing which overlooks the distinction between the world of immediacy and the world mediated by meaning.[87]

The world mediated by meaning is known not just by taking a look, but by the integrated personal and communal processes of understanding and judging the data of both internal and external experiencing that is proper to full human knowing. From this understanding of knowing, we can move to a recognition of reality as what is not only given in experience but also organized and extrapolated by understanding and affirmed by judgment and belief. Likewise, objectivity can be understood in terms of the criteria not only of eyesight and the other external senses but of experiencing, understanding, reasoning, and deciding.[88]

However, the essence of intellectual conversion is not in its philosophical explication and elimination of the "myth of the given" but in the prior personal performance of human knowing. The substance of intellectual conversion is the recognition and grasp of ourselves as knowers whose own self-transcending judgments, not some external norm, constitute the criterion of the real. In this sense intellectual conversion is a life-long task of learning and self-correction. When we are faithful to the transcendental precepts, we realize that our acts of understanding are always limited and conditional. Intellectual conversion is a daily, ongoing process of being attentive, intelligent, reasonable, and responsible.[89]

An experience of intellectual conversion is portrayed in the story of Jesus and the two disciples on the road to Emmaus (Luke 24:13-35). The disciples were debating about Jesus' passion and death when Jesus approached them. They did not recognize Jesus and were amazed that he seemed uninformed about the events they were discussing. They assumed everyone knew about the activities in Jerusalem this past week. They then proceeded to tell Jesus about the crucifixion, about the reports of his body being missing, and about a group of women describing a vision of angels who declared Jesus was alive.

Jesus responded: "What little sense you have!" They had failed to be attentive, intelligent, and reasonable in the experience! Then he proceeded to help them understand the scriptures which referred to his life and death so they could reason for themselves and obtain some insight into the meaning of the events of the past week.

As they reached Emmaus, the disciples asked Jesus to stay with them for a meal. When Jesus blessed and distributed the bread to them, the disciples recognized him. The recognition led to decision and action: "They got up immediately and returned to Jerusalem." Upon their reunion with the apostles, they recounted what had happened to them on the road and how they had come **to know** Jesus. These disciples were able to progress from a world of immediacy to a world mediated by meaning. With Jesus challenging them to be attentive, intelligent, and reasonable, they were able to utilize their own dynamics of human knowing and to recognize Jesus in the breaking of the bread.

Moral Conversion

Children are persuaded, cajoled, encouraged, ordered, compelled to do what is right. Usually as children grow into adults some degree of interiority develops. Lonergan describes interiority in terms of intentional and conscious acts on the four levels of experiencing, understanding, judging, and deciding. The fourth level, which presupposes, complements, and sublates the other three, is the level of freedom and responsibility. This level of freedom and responsibility includes the capacity for moral self-transcendence, in the sense of self direction and self control.[90]

The improper functioning of the fourth level is the uneasy or the bad conscience. The success of the fourth level is marked by the satisfying feeling that our duty has been done. The experience of moral self-transcendence is what Lonergan describes as moral conversion. This consists in opting for the truly good, choosing value against satisfaction when value and personal satisfaction conflict.[91] For example, it may be personally satisfying and gratifying to drive alone to work everyday. However, it is now known through environmental research that it is more ecologically valuable for us to car pool and use public transportation to decrease automotive emissions into the atmosphere.

Thus, moral conversion is a matter of deciding to act responsibly and to be governed fundamentally in our ethical activities by the criterion of what is truly good and worthwhile rather than by what merely satisfies the immediate demands for self-gratification. Moral conversion moves us into the vertical exercise of human freedom. We turn from a basically destructive, immoral way of existing and acting to a way of being and acting which is authentically worthwhile and truly good. This is a vertical exercise of human freedom because we are catapulted into a new sphere of moral existence, into a new world of authentic value.[92]

To journey down the road of moral conversion, several concepts need to be developed. These concepts include:

personal development, self-transcendence, authenticity, the development and discernment of feelings, and the ongoing aspect of moral conversion.

These concepts are the interwoven threads that make up the fabric of moral conversion.

Personal development is essential to moral conversion. Moral conversion presupposes some significant level of affective and intellectual development, although moral conversion should be seen as independent of religious and intellectual conversion. In fact, to be understood adequately moral conversion must be interpreted in the concrete context of personal development. For Lonergan, personal development is a process of self creation. This self creation and self development comprise the personal realization of the human spirit for self-transcendence.[93]

The capacity for self-transcendence is constituted by the transcendental notions. These transcendental notions are questions for experience, intelligence, reflection, and deliberation. Self transcendence moves us beyond ourselves. We live in a world and have horizons just in the measure that we are sensitive and not locked up in ourselves. Once we are sensitive to our environment, we ask questions and this questioning is unrestricted.[94]

First, there are questions for intelligence. We ask what and why and how and what for. Then follow questions for reflection whereby we move beyond imagination and guesswork, idea and hypothesis, theory and system. We ask whether or not a hypothesis really is so or really could be so. At this level, self-transcendence takes on a new meaning. For a judgment that a hypothesis is true signifies **not** what appears to us or what we think or wish, but what really is so.[95]

Still such self-transcendence is only cognitive and is in the order not of doing but only of knowing. However, on the final level of questions for deliberation, self-transcendence becomes moral. Moral self-transcendence is the possibility of benevolence, beneficence, and honest collaboration. Moral transcendence moves us from our animal habitat and enables us to become contributing members of the human society. This self-transcending movement commits us to becoming better persons than we presently are. Central to this process of self-transcendence is the fact that by deliberation, evaluation, decision, and action, we can know and do, not just what pleases us, but what is truly good and worthwhile.[96]

Recognizing what is truly good and worthwhile is a lengthy process which includes intellectual and affective development. A normative, personal conscience is never given as an accomplished fact. Moral conscience must be developed over time. We gradually grow in knowledge and slowly develop our responses to value. And as we develop, we are left to freely exercise an ever increasing movement toward authenticity.[97]

Precisely in this developing drive toward authenticity lies the possibility of moral conversion. Within this long and gradual process of personal becoming and increasing autonomy, we reach a crucial point. We discover that at this fourth level of conscious activity our own judging and deciding affect ourselves no less than the objects of our judgments and decisions. We are ultimately responsible for what we make of ourselves and our choices are crucial in the process of becoming authentic persons.[98]

This fourth level of deciding is the principle of self creation and is related to the proper functioning of the first three levels. This level fulfills its responsibility or fails to do so in the measure that we are attentive or inattentive in our experiences, that we are intelligent or unintelligent in our investigations, that we are reasonable or unreasonable in our judgments. The emergence of the fourth level of deliberation, evaluation, and choice is a slow process that begins between the ages of three and six. Still this is only the initiation of the ongoing process of human authenticity. We have to discover for ourselves that we have to decide what our destiny is to be. In other words, we have to prove ourselves equal to that specific moment of existential decision when it becomes clear that: "I am responsible for making the right choice in this situation." Plus we have to keep on choosing authenticity in all subsequent decisions.[99]

Human authenticity is not some pure quality or some serene freedom from all oversights, all misunderstandings, all mistakes, all transgressions. Rather human authenticity consists in a withdrawal from unauthenticity, and the withdrawal is never a permanent achievement. This withdrawal is ever precarious, ever to be achieved anew. Authenticity is an ongoing process of uncovering more oversights, acknowledging further failures to understand, correcting other mistakes, repenting of more deeply hidden sins. Authenticity is a continuing withdrawal from unauthenticity because every successful separation only brings to light the need for still further withdrawals.[100]

This alertness to authenticity puts us in a mode of healthy tension because authenticity is a matter of being obedient to the transcendental precepts of being attentive, being intelligent, being reasonable, and being responsible. This obedience entails facing questions. Modern psychologists have kept many neurotics bound in their neuroses by suggesting that all tension in consciousness is unhealthy. But the real psychic illness is to ignore, deny, or avoid the pressure of obeying the transcendental precepts that constitute authenticity.[101]

Some life tensions are resolved by choosing. The matter is decided and resolved for good or for ill. The situation is laid to rest. In contrast, existential tension is not resolved by choosing, because there is no absolute certainty whether good or ill will come of the choices. This heightened tension raises a fundamental question, because the reality slowly dawns on us that there is a basic decision to be made. Will we accept a life of existential tension, of being attentive, intelligent, reasonable, and responsible, or will we reject it? Is a lifetime of moral uncertainty and continuous struggle with ethical questions worthwhile, or might it be better to keep the tension at bay? The pressure can be kept at a distance in two ways:

1. by surrounding ourselves with good behavior we are fairly sure of; and

2. by forbidding our wonder and questioning to venture into areas where ethical questions and potential failures are almost certain.[102]

In contrast to negating questions, if we embrace the healthy tension inherent in being attentive, intelligent, reasonable, and responsible we set themselves on the journey of authenticity. Thus we affirm our own personal responsibility in judgments of value.

Lonergan explains that three components unite in the judgments of value. First, there is knowledge of human reality. Secondly, there are intentional responses to values. Thirdly, there is the initial thrust toward moral self-transcendence constituted by the judgment of value itself. The third component, judgment of value, presupposes knowledge of human life, of human possibilities, and of the probable consequences of projected courses of action. When there is insufficient knowledge, opinions are likely to be expressed in idealism and naivete, that is, in lovely proposals that lack a sound base and often do more harm than good.[103]

In the judgment of value, knowledge alone is not enough and must be combined with feelings. While everyone has some measure of moral feelings, these feelings must still be cultivated, enlightened, strengthened, refined, and criticized. The development of knowledge and moral feelings leads to an existential discovery of ourself as a moral being. The realization dawns that we not only choose between courses of action but, by our choices, make ourselves authentic or unauthentic human beings. With that discovery, there emerges in consciousness the significance of personal value and the meaning of personal responsibility. Judgments of value are revealed as the door to fulfillment or to loss. As authentic persons, we realize that our own individual conscience provides the criteria for judgments of value. The responsibility to utilize our own conscience in judgments of value cannot be relegated to others.[104]

Although feelings are not the final word in the judgment of value, they are the initial movement within us towards a value judgment. Also once a judgment is made, feelings consolidate judgment and give focus to attention, intelligence, reason, and responsibility. Feelings, and not thoughts, give an initial response to the worth of things. For example, we make a difficult phone call. The initial response is a feeling which might be one of relief, joy, disbelief, anger, frustration, or a combination of these. Later we reflect on the feelings and their possible meaning. Consequently, our feelings, assisted by our thoughts, elicit the cooperation of all consciousness in concrete moral action. However, both responsible and irresponsible people attend to their feelings and suppress some in favor of others. Therefore, a personal conscience should not be thought of as some list of right things to do hidden in our moral psyche. Conscience is rather a system in which our feelings, knowledge, skills, value judgments, and decisions are organized to work together.[105]

This organization is a developmental process and tends to head in either one or two possible directions, either towards the truly good or towards the merely satisfying. For example, boredom to restless adolescents might impel them to jump into the car and head for the nearest movie theater or shopping center. Boredom to responsible adults, aware of the transcendental precepts, will challenge them to be attentive to the feeling and process its meaning to come to a deeper understanding of the experience prior to making a trustworthy decision. Consequently, as responsible persons, we gradually organize our feelings not only towards values as opposed to mere satisfactions, but towards some values as more important than others. We learn to rank our various affective reactions to the objective good.[106]

To recognize the different quality of these affective movements is no easy matter. In discerning feelings, Dunne proposes that "a fully developed conscience dips back into past experience and remembers a few archetypical experiences of moral self-transcendence."[107] In other words, as authentic persons, we store up a memory of deeds which we consider good, and we also learn to remember a specific combination of feelings and images which proved the very real and immediate moral criteria by which we made decisions.[108]

Furthermore, we have learned to associate specific feelings with certain deeds by watching someone else act morally and by feeling our hearts touched; for example, observing others working for civil rights, building homes for destitute families, rescuing passengers from a sinking ship. Or perhaps, despite the personal odds facing us, we acted justly and earned a certain taste for justice and began from that day to depend on our newfound experience of justice. In other words, the transcendental precept, be responsible, is mediated to us to a large extent by the memory of a few key value judgments and their associated feelings. For authentic persons, these symbolic memories begin to embody the actual ground of our own morality and these remembrances encourage moral choices in other times and places under different circumstances.[109]

The choice of ourselves as the free and responsible creators of value is not forced. Indeed, this option can be a difficult decision to make and accept. But once made, this decision establishes an entirely new personal horizon. This horizon is specified by value as the criterion of decision and choice, and ultimately as the criterion of our very own way of life. Of course, even before this discovery and choice of ourselves as responsibly free and the consequent reorientation of our priorities and values, we have been developing and creating ourselves. The essential point of moral conversion is that after it occurs, this creation and development of self is open-eyed and deliberate.[110]

In light of this conversion and by virtue of it, "autonomy decides what autonomy is to be."[111] We choose ourselves as free and responsible; we now realize that our own choices and not an external norm molds and fashions us into morally good or bad persons.[112] As Paul explains in his letter to the Galatians (5:18, 22): "If you are guided by the Spirit you are not under the law. . . . The fruit of the Spirit is love, joy, peace, patient endurance. . . ."

Moral conversion and the consequent reorientation of priorities and values is an ongoing process. Additionally, continuous growth seems to be rare. There are the deviations occasioned by neurotic need. There are the refusals to keep on taking the plunge from settled routines to unexperienced but fuller modes of living. There are the mistaken endeavors to silence an uneasy conscience by ignoring, belittling, denying, and rejecting higher values. Our preference scales may become distorted and feelings may become soured. Bias may creep into thoughts and outlook, rationalization may creep into morals. We may come to hate what is truly good and to love what is really evil. This can happen to individuals, groups, nations, blocks of nations, all humankind.[113]

To prevent this decline, we have to keep developing our knowledge of human reality and potentiality. Consequently, we must be committed to:

1. continue distinguishing the elements of progress and of decline;

2. keep scrutinizing our intentional responses to values and our implicit scales of preferences; and,

3. continue listening to criticism and to protest.

We have to remain open to learn from others because this process is notoriously vulnerable to both error and malice. And yet this process is also responsive to the transcendental precepts:

be attentive,
be intelligent,
be reasonable,
be responsible.

When these are obeyed, error and malice are gradually overcome and the truly good gradually emerges.[114]

The transcendental precepts function to prevent decline as attention uncovers a problem. Intelligence produces explanations of the nature of the problem and suggests solutions. Next, reason tests the explanations and the suggestions to make sure the options are realistic. Finally, responsibility evaluates the costs and benefits to all concerned and applies the best available solution. This is how we can enhance situations. The improved situation, of course, has its own problems, but they are fewer in number. And the process continues because being moral means being creatures made to care for others. Being moral is fundamentally being in action for another. Being moral demands a commitment to true needs. As moral persons we have to discern what we really need and not merely drift with the winds of desire. Moral conversion aims to accomplish this discernment and often necessitates placing the good of others before our personal desires.[115]

The vigorous conscience of the morally converted continually directs the intelligence to discover how to share, how to welcome, how to enhance the lives of others. That is why authentic people are outraged at the sort of moral reasoning that claims to find certain circumstances in which deceit, wife or child abuse, murder, or war could ever be classified as "moral." These atrocities are nothing but the terrible price exacted for a long season of immorality in our world.[116]

In summary, moral conversion includes the following components:

1. personal development in which increasing knowledge and affective development is essential. There is a continued growth of self and realization of the need for transcendence.

2. self-transcendence which is constituted by questions for experience, intelligence, reflection, and deliberation. There is a desire and action to grow and develop, to become a better person.

3. authenticity in which we realize we are ultimately responsible for what we make of ourselves. Our choices and decisions are crucial in the process. We must be obedient to the transcendental precepts to be attentive, be intelligent, be reasonable, and be responsible for we are ultimately responsible in our judgments of value.

4. awareness of our feelings and the realization that feelings must be cultivated, educated, refined, and criticized. We

remember specific moments when deeds and feelings merged together in an experience of morality.

5. moral self-transcendence in which we choose ourselves as free and responsible. Benevolence, beneficence, and honest collaboration are possible because we discover how to share and enhance the lives of others and are committed to true needs and not merely to drifting with the winds of personal desire.

6. an ongoing process in which conscience is developed over time. In addition, conscience is seen as a system in which feelings, knowledge, skills, value judgments and decisions are organized to work together for the growth of self and the advancement of others.

These points are the crucial steps along the journey of moral conversion. This journey demands that we transcend ourselves; put the needs of others ahead of our personal desires; continue educating our consciences and feelings; struggle with discerning feelings to ascertain where the feelings are originating and leading; take responsibility for our choices; embrace authenticity and realize we are ultimately responsible for our own decisions. This is an excursion only to be made by those who are committed to growing personally and to enabling others to develop to their God-given potential.

The Scriptures (Exodus 19 and 20) offer some insight into moral conversion through the covenant on Mt. Sinai. God brings Israel out of Egypt so that the people can freely enter into the Sinai covenant. The covenant of Sinai was no mere business contract to be observed literally and for a limited time. Neither was the covenant a check list for measuring their worth before God. This covenant was given to the Israelites by a loving God seeking a loving response. At the heart of the covenant was the call to freely reach out to God and others. This covenantal call, to freedom and responsibility, developed over many centuries especially through the words of the prophets. Because the covenant demanded relationship and response, the prophets challenged the Israelites to remember the covenant and to put the needs of others, especially the poor and oppressed, before their own personal desires. The prophets attempted to educate and sensitize the consciences and feelings of the Israelites. And the prophets reminded the Israelites that they must accept responsibility for their own actions. The Israelites were ultimately responsible for their own destinies. They had to decide what they were to make of themselves.

"Today I have set before you life and prosperity, death and doom. If you obey the commandments of the Lord, your God, which I enjoin on you today, loving God, walking in God's ways, and keeping God's decrees, you will live and grow numerous. The Lord, your God, will bless you in the land you are entering to occupy. . . . Today I call heaven and earth to witness against you. I have set before you life and death, the blessing and the curse. Choose life, then, that you and your descendants may live" (Deut. 30:15-20).

Religious Conversion

The foundational event and process of religious conversion is God's gift of love flooding human hearts. This conversion occurs when we fall in love with God; when we realize we are individually and uniquely loved by God. Through religious conversion, we embrace the supreme value as God and see other values as God's expression of this love in the world.[117]

Religious conversion makes us who we are and is operative at every level of our existence. A basic consciousness develops which overflows into our imagining, experiencing, understanding, judging, deciding, believing and acting. This conversion is at the root of the understanding that we have of ourselves. The experience of God's love in religious conversion creates a basic consciousness in us which enables us to appreciate all as gift from God. This consciousness impacts how we view ourselves, our situation, our role in the human condition.[118]

Religious conversion, as the gift of God's love flooding the our hearts, is an experience of the indwelling of God's unrestricted acceptance and favor. This indwelling of God's love occurs simultaneously with the discovery of our true self. Thus, religious conversion is the discovery of self as worthwhile and significant because we exist in God's unconditional love. God does not love us because we are important and valuable; we are important and valuable because we are loved by God.[119] This is a sublime shift in consciousness against the cultural norm which emphasizes the need to earn another's love and respect.

Religious conversion is the reality of personal transformation that spontaneously produces effects. Being in love with God leads us to such judgment of fact as: God's own Spirit is indeed at work in every person. Being in love with God leads us to a more effective intelligence. Like the little children in the gospels (Matt. 20:14; Luke 18:16), we become more able to ask the how and why questions which most adults are hesitant to ask. Being in love with God leads us to a transformed attentiveness. We see all data as information on God. The world is charged with the glory of God and we are attentive to this glory in a wondering and loving way.[120]

Furthermore, we respond by loving the Lord God with our whole heart, whole soul, with all our mind and all our strength. This religious loving is without conditions, qualifications, and reservations. There is a movement into a deeper union with the Lord manifested by an increased simplicity and passivity in prayer. The gift of God's love occupies the ground and root of our intentional consciousness. We are ready to deliberate, judge, decide, and act with the easy freedom of those who do all good because they are in love. And, indeed, the experience is one of being grasped by ultimate concern, an experience of falling in love and of surrendering ourselves to the Beloved. This self surrender is not a single act; it is a dynamic state that is prior to and forms the rationale for subsequent acts.[121]

The experience of being loved by God calls us not only to self surrender, but also to self transcendence. We are affectively self transcendent, according to Lonergan, when the isolation of our individualism is broken, and we spontaneously act not just for self but for the good of others as well. When we experience falling in love, our love is embodied not just in this or that act or even in many series of acts, but in a dynamic state of being in love. Such being in love is the concrete first principle from which the affective life flows: desires and fears, joys and sorrows, discernment of values, decisions and deeds. Religious conversion as falling in love is a radical transformation of our life which turns our very self and shifts our orientation from an absorption in personal interests to concern for others.[122]

Falling in love with God imbues us with a new appreciation of the value of other persons, not for what they can do nor for how attractive they are, but for their inherent value as human beings. In light of their worth as persons, we are concerned about others and reach out to them. As growth in love occurs, we learn to be touched by even the most peculiar and grotesque persons and to allow ourselves to be enveloped by God present within all people. Through faith, we discover the profound mystery of others and are able to make loving commitments to them which last a lifetime.[123]

Religious conversion has a dual dimension which comprises both passion and commitment in self-sacrificing love. Religious conversion belongs to the interior world of feeling, that is, we fall in love; but this conversion is not simply a matter of passion. Religious conversion requires a deliberate decision on our part. We must consciously commit ourself to the Beloved. However, this commitment is no ethereal, disembodied act of will. Religious conversion is a transformation of our whole person which involves both intuitive passion and deliberate commitment.[124]

We fall in love because love is passionate. This passion is experienced as an unreflective desire to give of self to the Beloved without thought of personal cost. There is a certain passivity and helplessness originating and existing beyond and outside the control of our reflectively conscious self. It is as though the music is playing, the dance has begun, and we realize we are being led by Another to the sound of a new melody. This is an important experience because unless we passionately fall in love and unreflectively desire to give of self, we can only expect our decision to love the Other, though sincere, to be superficial at best. This love will image as a beautifully crafted, highly polished veneer, unlikely over the long term to stand up under the constant pressure of tough, everyday use. Due to its shallow roots, the seedling will eventually be scorched, will wither and die (Matt.13:4-7).[125]

Experience suggests not that religious conversion merely happens, but just the opposite. The possessiveness of the self's needs, not self-giving love, dominates us in the ordinary course of things. Our foremost, natural tendency is the desire to lead in the dance and not to be led by the Other. Consequently, religious conversion occurs not as an ordinary matter of course, but only as the extraordinary realization of God's unrestrictive acceptance and favor. We realize at the very core of our being that we are significant because we are loved unconditionally and eternally by God. Such a realization enables us to let go of obsessive concern for our own needs and to reach out in intimate love and generative care of others.[126] Such letting go brings a radical peace to us that the world cannot give – "Peace is my gift to you; I do not give it to you as the world gives peace. Do not be distressed or fearful" (John 14:27). The focus of the converted has moved from obsessive concern with self to a love of others that strives to bring about the Kingdom of God in the here and now.[127]

While religious conversion binds us to God in a more profound way, this conversion also reveals to us the unfathomable mystery of God and what a profound difference still remains between God and us. In our essence, we are creature before the Creator! Unless both this closeness and distance are present in the relationship, the peace is illusory and will not embrace this healthy, divine tension between the immanence and transcendence of God.[128]

This relatedness to God in religious conversion places us in a dialectical position. This dialectic means that we are challenged to embrace authenticity and to withdraw from unauthenticity. Religious authenticity allows faith, hope, and charity to realize what attention, intelligence, reason, and responsibility do not visualize by themselves. Our withdrawal from unauthenticity is never complete and is always precarious. The task of repentance and conversion is a life-long process. We need to pray daily to be forgiven for our transgressions against others and to forgive the transgressions of others against us. This is the journey of conversion, of daily death to self. While we may find the traveling difficult, religious conversion imbues the heart with the energy to put forth the effort and to endure the hardship involved in undergoing and implementing moral and intellectual conversion.[129] Through this process, love will be manifested by the wild flowers which erupt through the cracks in the cemented pathways of our lives.[130]

The following schema presents the dimensions of religious conversion and the scripture references that illustrate their presence in King David, one of the major figures of the Old Testament who reigned about the twelfth century B.C.E. David was chosen as an example of religious conversion because one of the most significant theological contributions of the Old Testament is found in the oracle of Nathan (2Sam. 7:4-17). In this passage, David is promised an eternal dynasty, and this promise becomes the basis for the development of royal messianism. David was also selected because so much of his life and various aspects of the spiritual journey are recorded in the Books of Samuel and in the Psalms.

Through David's story, we are able to see the following elements of religious conversion.

1. God initiates the relationship with David and there follows an outpouring of God's love into David's heart.

2. There is a realization by David that he is uniquely loved by God and this love affects David at all levels.

3. As David grows in this relationship with God, he experiences increased simplicity in prayer and a deeper realization that all is gift.

4. David is aware of the profound difference between God and himself, and with Nathan's help David realizes his need for repentance and for ongoing conversion.

The following schema of scripture references elucidates these aspects of religious conversion.

Dimensions of Religious Conversion Present in David's Life

Experiences God initiating and inviting the person into a unique relationship.	1 Sam. 17:37; 2 Sam. 7:9, 11; Ps. 16:8-11; Ps. 45:11-12
Experiences God's love flooding the heart.	2 Sam. 7:11; Ps. 16:8-9; Ps. 18:2-3, 20
Sees self as uniquely loved by God.	2 Sam. 7:11; Ps. 4:9; Ps. 10:1; Ps. 23; Ps. 27:1
Realizes that God is the supreme value.	2 Sam. 7:11; Ps. 13:6; Ps. 16:1-2
Sees other values as God's expression of love in the world.	2 Sam. 7:11-16; Ps. 8:4-5; Ps. 24:1-2; Ps. 33:5
God's love affects us at all levels:	
Imagining	Ps. 37:4 a; Ps. 139:1-2
Experiencing	Ps. 33:1; Ps. 131:1-3
Understanding	Ps. 25:4; Ps. 27:11; Ps. 73:16-17; Ps. 119:33
Judging	Ps. 32:8; Ps. 119:34
Deciding	Ps. 37:5-6; Ps. 119:35; Ps. 139:22-24
Believing	Ps. 37:7a; Ps. 119:10-11; Ps. 138:7-8
Acting	Ps. 40:8-9; Ps. 128:1

Sees God's Spirit at work in other people.	2 Sam. 7:19; Ps. 18:50-51; Ps. 33:13-15
Is able to ask questions.	2 Sam. 7:18; Ps. 43:5 a; Ps. 27:1
Sees all data as information on God	2 Sam. 7:21-24; Ps. 19:1-5
Experiences a deeper passivity and simplicity in prayer.	Ps. 6:10; Ps. 22:2-3
Realizes all is gift.	2 Sam. 7:18; Ps. 8; Ps. 67:7-8; Ps. 104
Experiences self as valuable because loved by God.	2 Sam. 7:19-20; Ps. 40:12; Ps. 103:1-5
Desires to transcend self, to be concerned about others.	2 Sam. 7:25; Ps. 16:3; Ps. 31:24 a; Ps. 40:11
Is able to be touched by even the most peculiar persons.	2 Sam. 18:1-5; Ps. 19:1-5
Experiences an unreflective desire to lose self in the Beloved.	Ps. 27:7-8; Ps. 34:2
Experiences reflective desire and commitment to give self to the Beloved.	Ps. 25:1; Ps. 27:4; Ps. 31:6; Ps. 62:2-3, 6-7
Is aware of the profound difference between God and self; is creature before the Creator.	2 Sam. 7:20, 28-29; Ps. 8:6-10; Ps. 18:31; Ps. 24:8-10

Sees religious conversion as a life-long process.	Ps. 19:12-13; Ps. 51
Realizes ongoing need for repentance.	2 Sam. 12:13, 20; 2 Sam. 24:10, 25; Ps. 19:14-15; Ps. 25:7, 11; Ps. 51; Ps. 73:14; Ps. 85:2-4

The scriptural examples given at the end of each section on conversion are offered as concrete examples of the elements present in each dimension of intellectual, moral, and religious conversion. These illustrations can be utilized by novice directors to discern which dimension of conversion needs to be emphasized in the spiritual journey of a novice.

The differentiation present in Lonergan's three dimensions of conversion enables the director to be sensitive to the unique and progressive growth of each novice. This differentiation meets the novices where they are along life's journey and offers them the opportunities and life experiences needed to continue to transcend themselves in their experiencing, understanding, judging, deciding, and loving. Through these examples and similar images, formation personnel can emphasize those elements of conversion essential for each novice.

Summary of Conversion

Conversion involves a new understanding of oneself because, fundamentally, conversion brings about a new self to be understood. Intellectual conversion frees us from confusing the criteria for knowledge in the world of immediacy with the criteria for knowledge in the world mediated by meaning. Moral conversion frees us to become motivated primarily by values and not by personal satisfactions. Religious conversion frees us to love God with all our heart, soul, mind, and strength; and impels us to love others.[131]

Conversion is taking off the old person and putting on the new and this is not just an expansion of a prior mode but the beginning of a new mode of living. Besides the beginning, there is also the consequent growth. Our development may me marred by few or by many relapses. The relapses may be successfully corrected, or they may leave their traces in small or grave defects. Because of its developmental nature, conversion is an ongoing process. Just as the flower turns its face to catch the sun to draw upon its energy, we must always be turning to God.[132]

As an ongoing process, conversion calls us to persist in being attentive, intelligent, reasonable, responsible, and loving. On the **level of attention**, we continue to experience ourselves as open to all possibilities. On the **level of intelligence**, we continue to ask questions that explain how or why, with the expectation that particulars will be understood. On the **level of judgment**, we continue to affirm or deny the explanation and to embrace what is real in a world mediated by meaning. On the **level of decision**, we continue to take responsibility for our actions and to strive for the truly good. On the **level of love**, we continue to realize we are uniquely cherished by God and to respond by loving God with our whole being and by embracing others in this love relationship.[133]

In essence there is only one conversion because religious conversion forms the basis for intellectual and moral conversion. God's gift of love is free and is not conditioned by our human knowledge or by our ethical behavior. Rather, this gift is the conviction that leads us to seek knowledge of God and to choose what is truly good. Religious conversion provides the real criterion by which all else is to be judged. To be converted religiously is to give oneself up to God's love flooding the heart and to subordinate everything to this love. When we are caught in the web of this love, we seek the highest value for others. This love is the catalyst that moves us to wake up and be attentive, to wonder and be intelligent, to reflect and be realistic, to deliberate and be responsible.[134]

Even though in essence there is only one conversion, the authentic Christian strives for the fullness of all three dimensions: intellectual, moral, and religious conversion. Without intellectual conversion, we tend to misapprehend not only the world mediated by meaning but also the word God has spoken within that world. Without moral conversion, we tend to pursue not what is truly good but what is only personally satisfying. Without religious conversion, we are radically desolate living without the full realization of God's unique love for us.[135]

In each conversion, transcendence is normative. There is an experience of awakening and we begin to be pushed and pulled beyond ourselves. This transcendent experience is a response to mystery. We realize that the quest is not primarily our pursuit of God, but rather God's pursuit of us. Thus, we are most powerful in our surrender to God. We experience ourselves as good and ask God to bring to life the goodness that is present within our questioning, acting, and loving.[136]

Lonergan has not, of course, uttered the last word on conversion. Some theologians have argued that Lonergan's notion of conversion is too general, underestimates the diversity of human cultures, is not sufficiently specific to theology, focuses on individualism and lacks the social and cosmic aspects constitutive of Christian conversion.[137] Lonergan himself and others have defended his theology against some of these criticisms.[138] While still others have utilized Lonergan's theology to further develop some of its aspects. Tad Dunne, Robert Doran, Bernard Tyrrell, Walter Conn have respectively developed the spiritual, psychological, and emotional aspects; Matthew Lamb has used some of aspects of Lonergan's work in Lamb's own theology of social transformation.[139]

As this debate over Lonergan's philosophy and theology continues, the fact remains that Lonergan's notion of conversion offers a foundational reality, the transformation of the person. This foundational reality is crucial to the time of the novitiate and thus offers one possible foundation in which to ground this period of religious formation.[140]

Conversion and the Novitiate Experience

The section on the novitiate experience emphasized the importance of the novice's personal transformation. As previously stated, one of the main purposes of the novitiate is to enable novices to gradually attain spiritual and human maturity. This maturity must be characterized by a growing self-knowledge which is manifested by an ability to face inner conflicts, to clarify motivations, to act responsibly and to make congruent and appropriate choices. Before novices are permitted to pronounce vows, they must have achieved that degree of human and spiritual maturity which will enable them to respond to the religious vocation with sufficient knowledge, personal responsibility, and free will.[141]

This human and spiritual maturity has been characterized by many religious as a profound conversion experience. Thus Lonergan's theological method, in which the notion of conversion and the transformation of the person play a central role, offers a potential foundation for the novitiate experience. As God is Truth, so conversion can awaken novices to the dynamic tension which urges them toward an ever fuller realization of the truth. As God is Good, so conversion can awaken novices to the dynamic tension which invites them toward an ever deeper desire for the good. As God is Love, so conversion can permeate novices with a peace beyond understanding, a peace the world cannot give. Conversion makes foundational the novices' discontent with the merely given and fills them with a hunger and thirst for the understanding, freeing, and passionate love of God.[142]

An added benefit of Lonergan's notion of conversion for the novitiate experience is its dimensionality. Since, the three dimensions are distinct, conversion can occur in one dimension without occurring in the other two, or in two dimensions without occurring in the third one. At the same time, the three dimensions are usually connected. Conversion in one leads to conversion in the others, and relapse in one leads to decline in the others.[143]

Conversion needs to be differentiated in order to meet novices where they are along life's journey and offer them what is necessary to continue their surrender to God. Each novice is different and has various and progressive levels of consciousness. Much time is needed to become familiar with each level and then to surrender that level to God.[144] With this schema, formation personnel can emphasize one aspect of conversion depending on the needs of the novice. Formation personnel can select classes, retreats, workshops, readings, and conference material which correspond to these needs and which encompass the dimensions of the conversion required by the novice.

Another advantage of this theology for the novitiate experience is the concept of sublation. According to Lonergan, sublation goes beyond what is sublated, introduces something current and distinct, and places everything on a new level. However, without interrupting or destroying what is sublated, this new base needs the old, includes it, preserves all its proper features and properties, and carries these features forward to a fuller realization within a richer context. The new goes beyond the old, but brings the old forward in an additive fashion.[145]

Sublation also needs to occur in the novitiate experience. Novices enter this experience with a history and culture; with personal, spiritual, and emotional capacities; with educational and vocational expertise.[146] Formation personnel are challenged to introduce a new lifestyle to the novices while preserving aspects of the novices' previous lifestyle.

Using the concept of sublation, formation personnel must assist the novices to take their old way of living and move the old way forward to a new level. However, this movement must be done in a way that includes the old, preserves all its proper features, and carries these features forward to a fuller realization within the context of living as a vowed religious. Rooted in their past, and moving toward their future, the novices will be enabled to find their direction from within themselves. They will begin to face their inner conflicts, to clarify their motivations, to act responsibly, and to make appropriate choices. They will discover an inner stability that will enable them to face ambiguity and insecurity. They will be able to struggle with the demands involved in assuming a congregational identity, because they are grounded in their own personal identity.[147]

Because of these advantages, Lonergan's notion of conversion offers a sound theological foundation for the novitiate. With such an infrastructure, the religious congregation has a solid base upon which to build a novitiate program which is both individualized to the needs of the novices and rooted in theology. Such a foundation will prevent the novitiate experience from being captured by any person, group, or movement within or outside the congregation and will prevent the novitiate experience from being turned in all different directions. Such a theological foundation will give a focus to the novitiate experience and will form the basis for the decisions and choices that are made regarding the daily functioning of the novitiate experience. Depending on the needs of novices, the three modes of conversion will assist them to grow in appreciation of these levels of consciousness and to mature in awareness of the transformation needed at each level.[148]

Through this ongoing process of moral, intellectual, and religious conversion, God will act to transform the novices' questioning, acting, and loving. Also through this process, novices will be adequately prepared to make a vowed commitment that is characterized by sufficient knowledge, personal responsibility, free will, and a deep, personal love of the Lord God.[149]

Through this dynamic process, novices will embark on their journey as vowed persons convinced of the need to be attentive, intelligent, reasonable, responsible, and loving. They will realize this is only a beginning; the seed has been planted and must be nourished for growth to occur. Persistence will be required all along the way because authentic fidelity results from the long-sustained exercise of attention, intelligence, reason, responsibility, and love.[150] However, the novices' experience of being uniquely loved by God will be the sustenance that will nourish them on their pilgrimage as vowed religious.

Notes

1. Thomas Gannon and George Traub, *The Desert and the City* (London: Macmillan Co., 1969) 18-19. Thomas O'Meara *Theology of Ministry* (New York: Paulist Press, 1983) 27. Jeanne Schweickert, *Who's Entering Religious Life?* (Chicago: National Conference of Religious Vocation Directors, 1987) 7.

2. Gannon and Traub, 17. Schweickert, 7, 115. *Perfectae Caritatis.*

3. *Lumen Gentium, Dogmatic Constitution on the Church*, #39-#43; *Perfectae Caritatis*, #3.

4. *Perfectae Caritatis*, #8-9. Jean Beyer, "Institutes of Apostolic Life," *Supplement to The Way* 8 (1969): 182. See also: George Aschenbrenner, "Active and Monastic: Two Apostolic Lifestyles," *Review for Religious* 45 (1986):653-668. Mary Ewen, Silvia Vallejo, and Paul Molinari, "Theological Reflections on Apostolic Religious Life," *Review for Religious* 43 (1984): 3-25. James Walsh, "Religious Communities: An Examination of their Apostolic Role," *Origins* 9 (1979): 397-409. Christiane Hourticq, "The Apostolic Religious Life—A Theological View," and Therese Revault, "Apostolic Religious Life—Challenges That Must Be Met," CRC Dossiers, 1-14.

5. Aschenbrenner, 657, 659.

6. Aschenbrenner, 658.

7. Aschenbrenner, 659-660.

8. *Perfectae Caritatis*, #8.

9. Ewen, Vallejo, Molinari, 13. Beyer, 189.

10. Aschenbrenner, 660-661.

11. Aschenbrenner, 661.

12. Aschenbrenner, 663.

13. Beyer, 191.

14. Aschenbrenner, 664-665.

15. Jean F. Godet, "Evangelical Life," Paper presented on Evangelical Life to the Sisters of St. Francis of Philadelphia, December 1984, 1.

16. Ad Hoc Committee, "Evangelical Life," Paper presented on Evangelical Life to the Sisters of St. Francis of Philadelphia, Immaculate Conception Province, March 1985, 2.

17. Godet, 1.

18. Ad Hoc Committee, 1.

19. Godet, 1-2.

20. Godet, 2-3.

21. Godet, 3.

22. Ad Hoc Committee, 6.

23. Godet, 5.

24. Aschenbrenner, 653-668. Province Delegates, "Evangelical Life," Paper presented on Evangelical Life to the Sisters of St. Francis of Philadelphia, March 1985, 2. Walsh, 400.

25. Bernard Tickerhoof, "Reflections on Religious Formation," *Review for Religious* 36 (1977): 58.

26. *Perfectae Caritatis*, #18.

27. Vatican Congregation for Religious and for Secular Institutes, "Renovationis Causam: Instruction on the Renewal of Formation for Religious Life" *The Way Supplement* 7 (1969): #2.

28. "Renovationis Causam," #9.

29. "Renovationis Causam," #4.

30. *Lumen Gentium*, #44; "Renovationis Causam," #13.

31. "Renovationis Causam," #4. Joan Faber, "Novitiate Formation," *The Way Supplement* 32 (1977): 64.

32. Faber, 64. Paul Molinari, "Religious Formation As It Looks Today," *Human Development* 1 (1980): 14.

33. "Renovationis Causam," #4. Faber, 64.

34. "Renovationis Causam," #15.

35. Paul Molinari, "The Novitiate: Initiation into Christ's Way of Life," *The Way Supplement* 41 (1981): 56.

36. Molinari, "Religious Formation As It Looks Today," 15. Donald Macdonald, "What is a Novitiate For?" *Review for Religious* 43 (1984): 334-335.

37. "Renovationis Causam" #5. Vatican Congregation for Religious and for Secular Institutes, "Contemplative Dimension of Religious Life," *Origins* 10 (1981): #20. Vatican Congregation for Religious and Secular Institutes, "Religious Life and Human Promotion," *Origins* 10 (1981): #32-33.

38. John Harriott, "A Note on Formation Personnel," *The Way Supplement* 8 (1969):247.

39. Faber, 64. Gerard Hughes, "Formation for Freedom," *The Way Supplement* 32 (1977): 44.

40. "Renovationis Causam," #21.

41. "Renovationis Causam," #21, #24.

42. Bruce Lescher, "Religious Formation: Beyond the Healing Paradigm," *Review for Religious* 42 (1983): 853-858. Patrick Moffett, "Two Models of Novitiate," *Human Development* 5 (1984): 23-26.

43. Moffett, 23-24.

44. Moffett, 24.

45. "Renovationis Causam," #11.

46. "Contemplative Dimension," #17-20. "Renovationis Causam," #15. Vatican Congregation for Religious and for Secular Institutes, "Religious Life and Human Promotion," *Origins* 10 (1981): #32-35.

47. Bernard Lonergan, "Grace After Faculty Psychology," *Curiosity at the Center of One's Life: Thomas More Institute Papers 1984*, ed. J. Martin O' Hara (Montreal: Thomas More Institute, 1987) 409. Lonergan, *Method* 267.

48. Lonergan, "Grace After Faculty Psychology," 409.

49. Lonergan, *Method in Theology* (Minneapolis: Winston Press, 1972).

50. Miriam Gramlich, "Ongoing Conversion and Religious Life" *Review for Religious* 40 (1981): 819.

51. Lonergan, *Method* 113.

52. Lonergan, *Method* 130. Tad Dunne, *Lonergan and Spirituality* (Chicago: Loyola University, 1985) 113.

53. Lonergan, *Method* 130.

54. Lonergan, *Method* 338.

55. Lonergan, *Method* 237-238.

56. Lonergan, *Method* 131.

57. Lonergan, *Method* 271.

58. Lonergan, *Method* 4, 6, 13, 17, 118, 238.

59. Lonergan, *Method* 130-131. Bernard Lonergan, "With Method in Theology," *Curiosity at the Center of One's Life: Thomas More Institute Papers 1984*, ed. J. Martin O"Hara (Montreal: Thomas More Institute, 1987) 395.

60. Lonergan, *Method* 243.

61. Lonergan, *Method* 238-242, 267. Hugo A. Meynell, *The Theology of Bernard Lonergan* (Atlanta: Scholars Press, 1986) 17. Lonergan, "Grace After Faculty Psychology" 406.

62. Michael Rende, "The Development of Fr. Bernard Lonergan's Thought on the Notion of Conversion," diss. (Marquette University, 1983) 280. Bernard Lonergan, *Collection: Papers by Bernard Lonergan*, ed. F.E. Crowe (New York: Herder and Herder, 1967) 222.

63. Lonergan, *Collection* 223.

64. Lonergan, *Method* 9.

65. Lonergan, "Since Writing Insight" 371. Dunne, 14.

66. Lonergan, "Since Writing Insight" 374. Dunne, 15, 31.

67. Lonergan, *Method* 13-20. Lonergan, "Since Writing Insight" 371. Dunne, 15-16.

68. Dunne, 25-27. Bernard Lonergan, *Understanding and Being: An Introduction and Companion to Insight, Halifax Lectures*, eds. Elizabeth Morelli and Mark Morelli (Toronto: Edwin Mellen Press, 1980) 133-155. Lonergan, *Method* 13-20.

69. Lonergan, *Method* 13-20. Dunne, 16, 33.

70. Lonergan, *Method* 11, 13-20. Dunne, 16-17, 19.

71. Lonergan, *Method* 13-20. Dunne, 16-17.

72. Lonergan, *Method* 10-11. Lonergan, *Collection* 225-226.

73. Lonergan, *Collection* 223.

74. Lonergan, *Method* 41-47. Dunne, 20.

75. Lonergan, *Method* 41-47. Dunne, 20-21.

76. Lonergan, *Method* 45. Dunne, 21.

77. Lonergan, *Method* 45-46. Dunne, 22.

78. Lonergan, *Method* 41-47, 78-79. Dunne, 22, 24. See Also: Elizabeth Kubler-Ross, *On Death and Dying* (New York: Macmillan, 1969).

79. Lonergan, *Collection* 228. Lonergan, *Method* 13.

80. Bernard Lonergan, *Third Collection: Papers by Bernard Lonergan*, ed. F.W. Crowe (New York: Paulist Press, 1985) 143.

81. Lonergan, *Third Collection* 143-144.

82. Bernard Lonergan, *Insight: A Study of Human Understanding* (London: Longmans, Green, and Co., 1957). W.F. Ryan, "Transcendental Reduction," *Creativity and Method: Essays in Honor of Bernard Lonergan*, ed. Matthew Lamb (Milwaukee: Marquette University Press, 1981) 407. Lonergan, *Method* 138-239. Meynell, *The Theology of Bernard Lonergan* 10.

83. Lonergan, *Method* 238-239. Lonergan, "With Method in Theology" 393. Lonergan, *Collection* 253. Hugo Meynell, *Introduction to the Philosophy of Bernard Lonergan* (New York: Harper & Row, 1976) 7.

84. Lonergan, *Method* 20, 53, 239-240. Ryan, 407. Dunne, 32.

85. Walter Conn, *Christian Conversion* (New York: Paulist Press, 1986) 121. Meynell, *Introduction to the Philosophy of Bernard Lonergan* 50-51.

86. Conn, 122.

87. Conn, 125. Rende, "The Development of Lonergan's Thought" 256.

88. Lonergan, *Method* 238-239. Conn, 125.

89. Conn, 125. Lonergan, *Method* 13, 20. Lonergan, "With Method in Theology" 400. Rende, "The Development of Lonergan's Thought" 141, 254.

90. Lonergan, *Method* 121, 240. Lonergan, "With Method in Theology" 393, 400. Bernard Lonergan, "Since Writing Insight," *Curiosity at the Center of One's Life: Thomas More Institute Papers/84*, ed. J. Martin O'Hara (Montreal: Thomas More Institute, 1987) 371.

91. Lonergan, *Method* 121, 240. Lonergan, "Grace After Faculty Psychology" 402, 406.

92. Lonergan, *Method* 240. Bernard Tyrrell, "Passages and Conversions," *Creativity and Method: Essays in Honor of Bernard Lonergan*, ed. Matthew Lamb (Milwaukee: Marquette University Press, 1981) 22.

93. Conn, 112-113. Lonergan, "Since Writing Insight" 372-373. Lonergan, *Method* 35.

94. Lonergan, *Method* 104-105.

95. Lonergan, *Method* 104. Lonergan, "With Method in Theology" 394.

96. Lonergan, *Method* 35, 104-108. Lonergan, "Since Writing Insight" 373. Lonergan, *Method* 35. Lonergan, "With Method in Theology" 393.

97. Conn, 113-114. Lonergan, *Method* 240.

98. Lonergan, *Method* 240. Lonergan, "Since Writing Insight" 372.

99. Lonergan, *Method* 121. Lonergan, "Grace After Faculty Psychology" 402.

100. Lonergan, *Method* 110, 252.

101. Dunne, 62. Lonergan, "Since Writing Insight" 371.

102. Dunne, 64-65. Lonergan, "Since Writing Insight" 383.

103. Lonergan, *Method* 38-39. Lonergan, "With Method in Theology" 393.

104. Lonergan, *Method* 38-39. Robert Doran, *Subject and Psyche: Ricoeur, Jung and Lonergan, The Search for Foundations* (Washington, D.C.: University Press of America, 1979) 59-65. Lonergan, "Since Writing Insight" 383. Rende, "The Development of Lonergan's Thought" 191.

105. Dunne, 70, 78. Lonergan, *Method* 38, 66-67.

106. Dunne, 78. Lonergan, *Method* 90, 114-115, 245.

107. Dunne, 79.

108. Dunne, 79.

109. Dunne, 79.

110. Conn, 115. Lonergan, "Grace After Faculty Psychology" 402, 406.

111. Bernard Lonergan, *Collection: Papers by Bernard Lonergan, S.J.*, ed. Frederick Crowe (Montreal: Palm Publishers, 1967) 242.

112. Rende, "The Development of Lonergan's Thought" 145. Lonergan, "Grace After Faculty Psychology" 406.

113. Abraham Maslow, *Toward a Psychology of Being* (Princeton, N.J.: Van Nostrand, 1962) 190. Abraham Maslow has found that self-actualization occurs in less than one percent (1%) of the adult population. Lonergan, *Method* 40, 243. Lonergan, "With Method in Theology" 400. Lonergan, 'Since Writing Insight" 376-377.

114. Lonergan, *Method* 240. Dunne, 91. Lonergan, "With Method in Theology" 393.

115. Dunne, 82, 87, 93. Lonergan, *Method* 237-244. Lonergan, "Since Writing Insight" 372-373. Lonergan, "With Method in Theology" 395.

116. Dunne, 83.

117. Lonergan, *Method* 105-107, 241, 242. Meynell, *The Theology of Bernard Lonergan* 10.

118. Lonergan, *Method* 53, 268. John Navone, "Bipolarities in Conversion," *Review for Religious* 40 (1981): 437.

119. Rende, "The Development of Lonergan's Thought" 247.

120. Lonergan, *Method* 242. Dunne, 138-140. See also: Rollo May, *Power and Innocence* (New York: Norton, 1969) 48-49 for a discussion of authentic innocence and pseudoinnocence.

121. Lonergan, *Method* 107, 240-242, 272. Lonergan, "With Method in Theology" 395.

122. Lonergan, *Method* 105-109. Walter Conn, *Christian Conversion* (New York: Paulist Press, 1986) 134-135.

123. Lonergan, *Method* 240-242. Dunne, 118-119, 137. Doran, 74.

124. Lonergan, *A Third Collection* 10. Conn, 148. Lonergan, *Method* 242.

125. Lonergan, *Method* 242. Conn, 149.

126. Lonergan, *Method* 241-242. Conn, 152. Rende, "The Development of Lonergan's Thought" 247.

127. Lonergan, *Method* 105.

128. Dunne, 127.

129. Lonergan, *Method* 118, 284. Lonergan, *A Third Collection* 9. Dunne, 129.

130. Dunne, 121. Meynell, *The Theology of Bernard Lonergan* 10.

131. Lonergan, *A Third Collection* 247-248.

132. Lonergan, *A Third Collection* 247. Michael Rende, "Class Presentation" (Spokane, Wash.: Gonzaga University, Spring 1988).

133. Dunne, 115-116. Lonergan, *Method* 240.

134. Lonergan, *Method* 338-340. Meynell, *The Theology of Bernard Lonergan* 17. Lonergan, *Method* 283-284. Lonergan, "With Method in Theology" 395. Dunne, 108, 112-113.

135. Lonergan, *A Third Collection* 248.

136. Lonergan, *A Third Collection* 131. Rende, "Class Presentation."

137. Meynell, *The Theology of Bernard Lonergan* 29-46. Charles Curran, "Christian Conversion in the Writings of Bernard Lonergan" *Foundations of Theology, Papers from the International Lonergan Congress, 1970,* ed. Philip McShane (Notre Dame: University of Notre Dame, 1972) 46-53.

138. Bernard Lonergan, "Bernard Lonergan Responds" *Foundations of Theology: Papers from the International Lonergan Congress, 1970,* ed. Philip McShane (Notre Dame: University of Notre Dame, 1972) 223-224. Meynell, "Objections to the Method" *The Theology of Bernard Lonergan* 29-46.

139. Robert Doran, *Psychic Conversion and Theological Foundations: Toward a Reorientation of the Human Sciences* (Chicago: Scholars Press, 1981). Robert Doran, *Psychic Conversion and Theological Foundations* (Chicago: Scholars Press, 1981). Matthew Lamb, *Solidarity with Victims* (New York: Crossroad, 1982). Conn, *Christian Conversion.* Dunne, *Lonergan and Spirituality.* Tyrrell, "Passages and Conversions." Bernard Tyrrell, *Christotherapy: Healing Through Enlightenment* (New York: Seabury Press, 1975). Bernard Tyrrell, *Christotherapy II: The Fasting and Feasting Heart* (Ramsey, N.J.: Paulist Press, 1982).

140. Rende, "The Development of Lonergan's Thought" 292. Gramlich, 819.

141. "Renovationis Causam, #4. Faber, 64.

142. Gramlich, 819. Rende, "The Development of Lonergan's Thought" 292.

143. Lonergan, *A Third Collection* 247.

144. Rende, "Class Presentation."

145. Bernard Lonergan, "Theology in a New Context" *Conversion* ed. Walter Conn (New York: Alba House, 1978) 19. Lonergan, *Collection* 228.

146. Faber, 57-61.

147. Faber, 60.

148. Lonergan, "Grace After Faculty Psychology" 499. Rende, "Class Presentation."

149. Rende, "Class Presentation." Faber, 64.

150. Lonergan, *A Third Collection* 9.

Chapter Three

Methodology

The first two chapters of this book presented background material from which the study was developed. This chapter describes the selection and description of the sample, the research design, the data collection procedures and the data analysis methods used in this study.

The purpose of this study was to explore the necessity of a theological foundation for the novitiate experience in light of the behaviors expected of a novice by the novice director upon the completion of the novitiate.

The study was undertaken to determine if there was a significant difference among the dimensions of conversion (intellectual, moral, and religious) emphasized in novitiate programs. The study was also done to determine if there was a significant difference between the variables encompassing the novitiate behaviors based on the dimensions of conversion described by Bernard Lonergan (intellectual, moral, and religious conversion) and the type of congregation (apostolic, monastic, and evangelical).

The study addressed the following research questions:

1. Is there a significant difference among the dimensions of conversion (intellectual, moral, and religious) emphasized in novitiate programs?

2. Is there a significant difference among apostolic, monastic, and evangelical congregations relative to the dimension of conversion identified in their novitiate programs?

3. What is the most important concept or behavior for a novice to learn and integrate into her/his own life by the end of the novitiate?

Description of the Subjects

The study was conducted among novice directors attending the National Congress of the Religious Formation Conference in New Orleans, Louisiana, in October, 1987. A questionnaire was given to these directors, and they were asked to complete the instrument during their days at the Congress and to return the questionnaire to the researcher before the Congress concluded.

Approximately 210 questionnaires were distributed and 150 (71.4%) questionnaires were returned in usable form. This sample size provided a 95 percent level of confidence with a five percent level of precision.[1]

The three graphs on the next pages describe the following:

Graph I presents the type of congregation of the participants;

Graph II presents the geographical location of the participants; and

Graph III details which of the participants functioned as part of a novitiate team and which of the participants did not function as part of a team.

Of these 150 participants, there were:

124 (82.7%) female novice directors; and
26 (17.3%) male novice directors.

Twenty-five percent of these directors were from congregations whose total membership amounted to more than 1200 members. The size of the congregations that the novice directors represented is displayed in Table I on page 72.

Type of Congregation of Participants

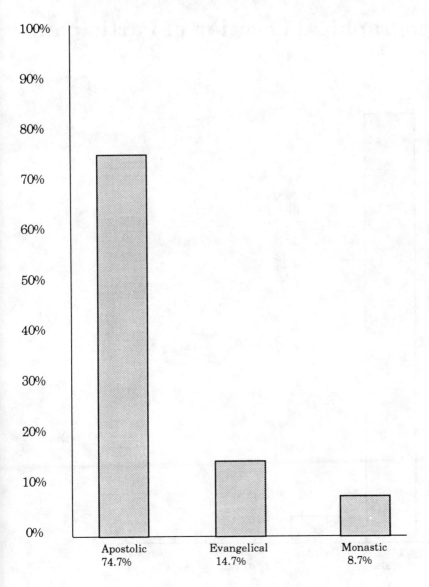

Graph I

Geographical Location of Participants

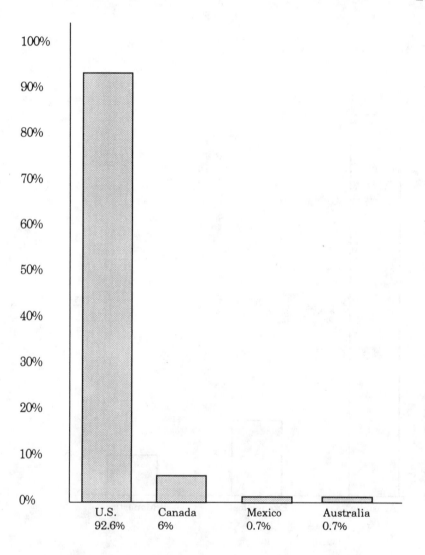

Graph II

Directors and Novitiate Teams

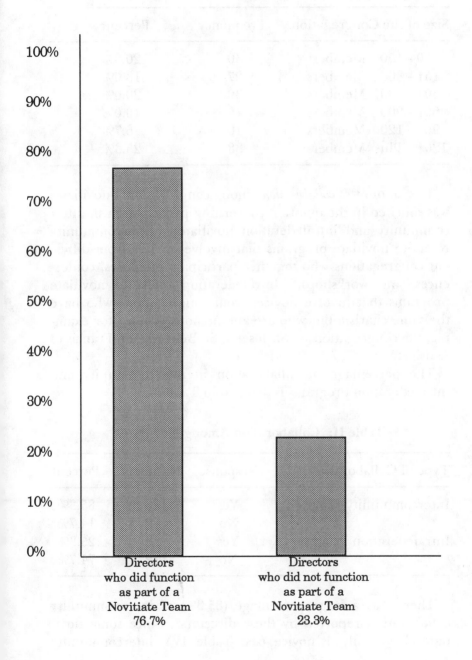

Graph III

Table I: Congregation Membership of Novice Directors

Size of the Congregation	Frequency	Percent
0 - 150 Members	30	20.0%
151 - 300 Members	27	18.0%
301 - 600 Members	30	20.0%
601 - 900 Members	15	10.0%
901 - 1200 Members	10	6.7%
1201 Plus Members	38	25.3%

The amount of *collaboration* among congregational novitiates was solicited in the question concerning participation in inter-community and intrafederation novitiates. Intercommunity refers to novitiate programs that involve novices from different congregations who together participate in classes, conferences, and workshops. Intrafederation refers to novitiate programs that involve novices from congregations who have the same charism but who are autonomous groups; for example, the congregations of St. Joseph, St. Benedict, St. Francis of Assisi, etc.

The percentage of collaboration in intercommunity and intrafederation programs is detailed in Table II.

Table II: Collaboration Among Novitiates

Type of Collaboration	Response	Number	Percent
Intercommunity Program	Yes	128	85.3%
	No	22	14.7%
Intrafederation Program	Yes	38	25.3%
	No	112	74.7%

There was a large percentage (85.3%) of intercommunity collaboration reported by these directors. Since some novitiates have only 1 novice (see Table IV), intercommunity

collaboration is almost an essential aspect of novitiate formation. This collaboration could offer support and assistance to
both novices and directors. Intercommunity collaboration
could also allow for pooling of resources among religious
congregations which would help to offset the over-all costs of
novitiate programs.

One director reported that his congregation had a program
that functioned among the provinces of his congregation.
This may have been true for other congregations as well
because this category was added during the Congress and the
direction to write it on the survey may not have been received
by all the participants.

These novice directors described the *length* of their
novitiates in the following ways. Most congregations (104 or
69.3%) had a novitiate which lasts for 24 months. Some
congregations (26 or 17.3%) had a novitiate which lasts for 12
months. A few congregations (7 or 4.7%) had a novitiate
which lasts for 18 months. One congregation (0.7%) reported
a novitiate which lasts for 9 months; and 2 congregations
(1.3%) reported a novitiate which lasts for 10 months. There
were single responses (0.7%) in the categories of 13 months, 14
months, 16 months, 20 months, and 21 months. There was 1
missing case.

Various types of *housing* for the novitiate were represented
in the responses. Seventy-one of the congregations (47.3%)
represented had their novitiates as autonomous houses. Forty
congregations (26.7%) had their novitiates as part of the
central administration house. Twenty-six congregations
(17.3%) had their novitiates as part of another house. Thir-
teen congregations (8.7%) had other arrangements for housing
the novitiate.

The *length of time* that these novice directors have been
engaged in formation work varied from 1 year to 21 years with
1 year having the highest frequency of 35 (23.3%). Table III
on page 74 presents these responses.

The responses concerning the *membership* of these novitiate
communities showed that many of them had final professed
members living in the novitiate houses. Most of the novitiates

Table III: Length of Time as Novice Director

Year/s as a Novice Director	Frequency of Response	Percent of Response
1	35	23.3%
2	19	12.7%
3	22	14.7%
4	16	10.7%
5	18	12.0%
6	13	8.7%
7	4	2.7%
8	7	4.7%
9	2	1.3%
10	3	2.0%
11	4	2.7%
12	2	1.3%
13	1	0.7%
14	3	2.0%
21	1	0.7%

had 2 to 4 final professed members residing in the novitiate community. Two final professed members were living in 26 (17.3%) of the novitiates. Three final professed members were living in 29 (19.3%) of the novitiates. Four final professed members were living in 19 (12.7%) of the novitiates. Most of the novitiates (108 or 72.0%) had no temporary professed members living in the novitiate community. Twenty-five (16.7%) of the novitiates had 1 temporary professed member in residence. The number of novices in residence in these novitiates is presented in Table IV on page 75.

This information on the large number of novitiates (31.3%) with only 1 novice in residence coincides with the data discussed in Chapter One on the decline in the number of women and men entering religious life since 1966.[2]

Most of the novitiates (98 or 65.3%) had no candidates in residence in the novitiate community. In this study, a candi-

Table IV: Number of Novices in the Novitiate Programs

Number of Novices	Frequency	Percent
3 Novices	16	10.7%
2 Novices	21	14.0%
1 Novice	47	31.3%
0 Novice	35	23.3%

date was defined as a person who is interested in becoming a member of a religious congregation, but who has not been formally accepted into the congregation's novitiate program. Twenty-seven (18.0%) had 1 candidate residing in the novitiate. Fourteen (9.3%) had 2 candidates in residence.

The *average age* of the final professed members living in the novitiate community house was 45 years. The average age of the temporary professed residing in the novitiate house was 30 years. The average age of the novice was 30 years. The average age of the candidates residing in the novitiate house was 25 years.

The novice directors described their theological schools or philosophies which formed the basis of their novitiate teaching in a myriad of ways. Table V on page 76 shows the responses that ranged from a frequency of 24 to a frequency of 2. These categories are not mutually exclusive.

There were also single response for the following schools or philosophies: Augustinian, Alphonsus Ligouri, Christian anthropology, Church-centered, French School (de Sales, de Paul, Berulle), George Aschenbrenner, John of the Cross, Passion Theology, Reality Therapy, Systematic Theology, Theresian, Theological Reflection Model.

The majority of these directors had received special education and training for their role as novice director. The type of education they received is displayed in Table VI on page 77.

Some of these respondents listed the program they had attended to receive their degree or certificate. These responses are enumerated in Table VII on page 77.

Table V: Theological School or Philosophy
of Novice Director

School or Philosophy	Frequency
Franciscan	24
Incarnational	21
Ignatian/Jesuit	14
Combination of Theologies	14
Process Theology	13
Creation Centered	12
Biblical/Scriptural	11
Liberation Theology (including feminism)	8
Holistic	6
Existential Philosophy	6
Conversion	6
Vatican II	5
RCIA	5
Benedictine	5
Psychological/Developmental Psychology	4
Apostolic Spirituality	4
Karl Rahner	4
Phenomenological	3
Monastic	3
Thomistic/Dominican	3
Bernard Lonergan	2
Catholic Spirituality	2
Experiential	2
Individualistic Approach	2
Paul Molinari	2

Table VI: Type of Education for the Role of Novice Director

Response	Frequency	Percent
Certificate or Degree/s	56	37.4%
Combination of Workshops and Degree/s	55	36.7%
Workshops only	23	15.3%
Life Experience	10	6.7%
Readings and Tapes	1	0.6%
No specific education	3	2.0%
No response	2	1.3%

Table VII: Formal Programs Specified

Name of the Program	Frequency
Institute of Religious Formation, St. Louis	24
Aquinas Institute of Theology, Duquesne University	8
Focus on Leadership, Gonzaga University	6
Christian Spirituality Program, Creighton University	5
Gregorian University, Rome	3
Institute of Spirituality and Worship, Berkeley	2
Masters of Pastoral Studies, Loyola University	2
University of Toronto, Canada	1
St. Bonaventure University, Franciscan Institute	1
Notre Dame University	1
University of San Francisco	1

The following summary statements can be made regarding this demographic data:

1. Seventy-four percent (74%) of the subjects who participated in the study were from apostolic congregations.

2. Eighty-five percent (85%) of the directors were involved in intercommunity collaborative efforts in novitiate formation.

3. Seventy-one percent (71%) of the directors had their novitiates in autonomous houses of their congregations.

4. Fifty percent (50%) of these directors had been novice directors for one to three years.

5. These directors were specially educated and trained for their roles. Eighty-nine percent (89%) had attended degree programs, certificate programs, or workshops in preparation for their ministries as novice director.

6. Most of the novitiates (65%) guided by these novice directors extended over a two year period.

7. Some novitiates (31%) had one novice in residence and a few (14%) had two novices in residence.

8. The ages of the novices participating in these programs were scattered with 28% of the novices being 25 to 35 years of age.

Design of the Study

This section focuses on a description of the variables, the instrument, the data collection, and the data analysis procedures used in this study.

The study examined the behaviors which the novice director considered important for a novice to manifest by the end of the novitiate. This variable was related to the type of congregation of the novice director which included apostolic, evangelical, or monastic.

The variables observed through this survey included:

1. the type of religious congregation: apostolic, evangelical, and monastic;

2. the dimensions of conversion: intellectual, moral, and religious.

The unit of analysis was the novice director. For the purposes of this paper, a "novice director" is defined as the person specifically chosen by a religious congregation to be responsible for the novitiate program of the congregation. As mandated by the Sacred Congregation for Religious and Secular Institutes, these directors are usually specially educated for their position through formal classes or through attendance at workshops focused on religious formation.[3] Since these directors are specially educated, they are familiar with the process of novitiate formation and with the process of growth and development expected to occur during this time.

After a careful review of the literature, Katie found that no prior instrument had been used in studying this topic. Therefore, the instrument used for the study was designed by her. The instrument developed was a self-administered, self-reporting, standardized survey (see Appendix A).

This type of instrument was developed for several reasons. First, the review of literature demonstrated a lack of statistical data on novitiate programs. Articles were written in religious journals each year about novitiate formation, but these were not based on research. Since there was no prior instrument developed, a survey seemed an appropriate method to explore the topic. The questionnaire could be completed privately, confidentially, and anonymously and thus would pose little threat to the participants.

Another reason for the utilization of a survey was the theory base of the questions. Lonergan's three dimensions of conversion were congruent with a survey format. Statements that describe these different dimensions could be incorporated into a survey format.

Also the survey could be self-administered which would allow the respondents to complete it at their own leisure. Since the survey was given out at a national conference, the respondents were able to choose their own time during the three day period to complete it. Distributing the survey at the Congress also made the instrument economical in terms of administering it to a group and receiving the responses in a short time period without having to incur extensive mailing costs.

A cover letter explaining the study was attached to each survey. The first section contained forty behaviors which described the different aspects of intellectual, moral, and religious conversion based on the theology of Lonergan. Using a scale of 1 to 7, where "1 = of no importance" and "7 = of great importance," the respondents had to rank the degree of importance that they would give to the behavior described in each statement being manifested by the novice upon completion of the novitiate. These data helped to determine, first, if there was a significant difference among the dimensions of conversion emphasized in the novitiate. Secondly, these data offered sufficient evidence to determine if there was a significant difference between the type of congregation and the form of conversion emphasized in the novitiate.

At the end of this section, the directors were asked to describe in three or four sentences their view of the most important concept or behavior for a novice to learn and integrate into his or her own life by the end of the novitiate. The responses to this question were used to answer the third research question: what is the most important concept or behavior for a novice to learn and integrate into his or her own life by the end of the novitiate?

The second section of the survey gathered general information about the congregation and novitiate program of each respondent. This information was used to describe the sample of participants, their novitiate programs, and their congregations.

The validity of the instrument and the reliability of the statements were created through two series of pilot testing which occurred in the Spring of 1987. Validity and reliability were also established through meetings with persons who had expertise in formation and in Lonergan's theology of conversion. Recommendations from these pilot tests, from Katie's dissertation committee, from Gonzaga University faculty, and from members of an instrument design class at Gonzaga University all contributed to the design and expansion of the survey instrument (see Appendix A).

As a result of these consultations and pilot tests, the statistical results on the reliability of the statements describing the different dimensions of conversion yielded high reliability coefficients.[4] The statements describing intellectual conversion had a reliability coefficient of 0.89; the statements describing moral conversion had a reliability coefficient of 0.90; the statements describing religious conversion had a reliability coefficient of 0.90. These reliability coefficients indicated that the three forms of conversion were being measured consistently and precisely with the instrument.

Data Collection Procedures

The survey (see Appendix A) was distributed to the novice directors attending the National Congress of the Religious Formation Conference in 1987. A special meeting was held with these directors during the Congress to solicit their participation in the study, to emphasize the importance of the study for religious formation, to assure anonymity, and to inform the participants that feedback regarding the study would be published at some future time. The format of the questionnaire was then explained and distributed.

A cover letter (see Appendix A) addressed to the novice directors was attached to the survey which explained the purpose, the various sections of the instrument, and a note of appreciation for their participation in the study. A table was set-up to receive the completed surveys and reminders were given to the participants throughout the Congress. If both a novice director and assistant director from the same novitiate program were attending the Congress, they were requested to collaborate in the completion of one survey.

Data collected by the questionnaire were entered into the Vax Mainframe Computer System at Gonzaga University, and the SPSSX program was used to analyze the data. Appendix B contains a copy of the data plan and the summary matrix design for this study.

Data Analysis

A repeated measures analysis was used to analyze the relationship among the dimensions of conversion for the first research question: is there a significant difference among the dimensions of conversion emphasized in the novitiate?

The statements from the questionnaire which described behaviors characteristic of the three dimensions of conversion are presented in Table VIII on pages 83-85.

A Multivariate analysis of variance was calculated to establish the relationship between the variables of types of congregation (apostolic, evangelical, and monastic) and the dimensions of conversion (moral, intellectual, and religious) for the second research question: is there a significant difference among apostolic, evangelical, and monastic congregations relative to the dimension of conversion emphasized in their novitiate programs.

Raw data from an open-ended question on the survey were analyzed for the third research question: what is the most important concept or behavior for a novice to learn and integrate into his or her own life by the end of the novitiate? The summation of the raw data from this question can be found in Appendix C. The results of the research follow in Chapter Four relative to this question as well as the other two research questions.

Table VIII: Statements from the Survey describing the Different Dimensions of Conversion

Statements on the survey describing aspects of intellectual conversion:

Number	Statement
2.	Seeks to know and understand self through his/her relationships with others.
5.	Experiences education as an ongoing and self-correcting process of learning.
8.	Utilizes and appreciates his/her intellectual abilities.
11.	Reflects on personal insights and assesses these insights to discover what is true in them.
14.	Seeks to know and understand other religions.
17.	Demonstrates confidence in her/his intellectual and rational processes.
20.	Sets goals and long-range plans for personal development.
23.	Strives to understand the history and charism of the congregation.
26.	Questions and reflects upon her/his daily life experiences.
29.	Can sensitively ask questions about the congregation's response to the gospel.
34.	Strives to increase his/her own knowledge and understanding of the world.
37.	Examines the meaning and relevance of Church teaching in his/her search for truth.
39.	Views long-range planning as important for the development of the congregation.

Table VIII: (continued)

Statements on the survey describing aspects of moral conversion:

Number	Statement
1.	Assumes responsibility for her/his own personal development.
4.	Strives to adopt a value system which forms the basis of his/her decisions.
7.	Reflects on various ethical systems in the development of his/her values.
10.	Bases decisions primarily on values and not on his/her personal satisfaction.
13.	Discerns those feelings which impact her/his values and judgments.
16.	Knows that moral conscience is developed over time.
19.	Discerns values in dialogue with self and others.
22.	Deals with her/his personal fears concerning the unknown.
25.	Owns his/her feelings and can constructively express these feelings to others.
28.	Takes responsibility for the development of her/his own moral conscience.
31.	Takes a personal stand on the values affirmed as important to self.
33.	Participates in various experiences and educational opportunities that will develop his/her feelings.
36.	Carefully examines the values which she/he has adopted.

Table VIII: (continued)

Statements on the survey describing aspects of religious conversion:

Number	Statement
3.	Shows a listening and receptive spirit in prayer.
6.	Demonstrates a strong trust in God's unconditional love for her/him.
9.	Experiences self as loving and being loved by God.
12.	Views intimate and loving relationships as needed for personal growth and development.
15.	Shows a willingness to deal with the ambivalent feelings normally present in love relationships.
18.	Knows that love involves judging, deciding, and choosing to love another.
21.	Seeks to discover her/his true self in relationship with God.
24.	Knows that God initiates and calls the person to a love relationship.
27.	Sees the necessity of growing more open and attentive to God's love for him/her.
30.	Fosters mutual respect and interdependence in his/her relations with others.
32.	Demonstrates that a deep, personal, and communal prayer life is essential to a relationship with God.
35.	Demonstrates a loving care for others.
38.	Experiences self as worthwhile and significant because he/she exists in God's unconditional love.
40.	Reaches out beyond self to others because God has become the center of her/his life.

Notes

1. Taro Yamane, *Elementary Sampling Theory* (New Jersey: Prentice-Hall, 1967) 398.

2. Granfield, 121.

3. Vatican Congregation for Religious and for Secular Institutes, "Contemplative Dimension of Religious Life," *Origins* 10 (1981): #20.

4. Dennis Hinkle, William Wiersma and Stephen Jurs, *Applied Statistics for the Behavioral Sciences* (Boston: Houghton Mifflin Co., 1979) 85.

Chapter Four

Research Results

The purpose of Katie's study was to explore the necessity of a theological foundation for the novitiate experience in light of the behaviors expected of a novice by the novice director upon the completion of the novitiate. Analyzing the results of the "Formation Survey" (Appendix A) comprised the methodology for the study. The results of the survey are organized in relation to the three research questions presented in Chapter One.

Research Question One

Is there a significant difference among the dimensions of conversion emphasized in the novitiate?

Findings

The test results showed that there was a normal distribution of scores for the statements on moral and intellectual conversion. However, the statements for religious conversion from the apostolic congregations were slightly skewed. Since the number of respondents was greater than thirty for the apostolic congregations (n = 111), the data were analyzed as they were without transformation because where n > 20 this assumption violation has quite small effects on the test conclusions.[1]

The assumption of equality of variance for the dependent variables of intellectual, moral, and religious conversion was met as validated by Cochrans' test. The assumption of equality of variance between the groups of monastic, apostolic, and evangelical congregations for all dependent variables combined was also met as validated by the Box M test.

Bartlett's test of sphericity was significant, p = .00. Therefore, we can assume that the variables were dependent on one
another, that they formed an identity matrix.[2] This conclusion was also validated in the correlation coefficients. Moral to
intellectual conversion had a correlation coefficient value of
.880. Moral to religious conversion had a correlation coefficient value of .803. Intellectual to religious conversion had a
correlation coefficient value of .755. According to Hinkle,
these correlation coefficient values would indicate high
positive correlations.[3]

There were 40 statements on the survey describing different
aspects of the 3 dimensions of conversion — intellectual, moral,
and religious conversion. The novice directors were asked to
rank each of the 40 statements using a range of 1 to 7, where
"1 = of no importance" and "7 = of great importance."
Through the utilization of this scale, the directors were
requested to indicate the degree of importance they would
give to the behavior described in each statement being
manifested by the novice upon the completion of the novitiate.

Based on the raw data from the survey, the mean scores and
standard deviation scores for the three conversion variables
from the entire sample are presented in Table IX.

**Table IX: Mean Scores and Standard Deviation Scores of
Conversion for the Entire Sample**

Dimension of Conversion	Mean	Standard Deviation
Religious	89.68	7.65
Moral	76.66	8.83
Intellectual	73.62	9.46

The mean scores indicate that the statements describing
aspects of religious conversion were given greater importance
by the directors. Moral conversion and intellectual conversion
were second and third respectively.

For the purpose of repeated measure analysis, an average
was taken on each form of conversion since there was an

unequal number of statements measuring each variable. Religious conversion was described in 14 statements; moral conversion was described in 13 statements; and intellectual conversion was described in 13 statements.

The repeated measures analysis for the dimensions of conversion (intellectual, moral, and religious) was found to be *significant* ($F = 183.965$; df = 2, 146; $p < .05$) by the Pillais test. The mean scores and standard deviation scores for each form of conversion utilizing the averages of the variables are presented in Table X.

Table X: Mean and Standard Deviation Scores for the Different Dimensions of Conversion

Dimension of Conversion	Mean	Standard Deviation
Religious	6.407	.542
Moral	5.900	.674
Intellectual	5.671	.722

There was also a significant difference in how the respondents scored comparatively on intellectual, moral, and religious conversion. Each conversion was significantly different from the other two dimensions of conversion ($p < .05$). The summary table describing these comparisons is presented in Table XI.

Table XI: Summary Table for the Comparisons of the Different Dimensions of Conversion

Dimensions of Conversion		Hypoth MS	Error MS	F
Moral	vs. Intellectual	3.87	0.059	65.49
Moral	vs. Religious	19.07	0.080	236.31
Religious	vs. Intellectual	40.12	0.1107	362.22

Research Question Two

Is there a significant difference among apostolic, evangelical, and monastic congregations relative to the dimension of conversion emphasized in their novitiate programs?

Findings

The test results were *not* significant related to the research question on the form of conversion (intellectual, moral, and religious) emphasized in novitiate programs and the type of congregation (monastic, apostolic, and evangelical). The multivariate analysis of variance for the type of congregation and intellectual, moral, and religious conversion was not found to be significant ($F = .06823$; $df = 6, 282$; $p > .05$).

However, the Univariate F test *was significant* ($df = 2, 142$; $p < .05$). The results of this test for the type of congregation and each form of conversion are presented in Table XII.

Table XII: Summary Table for Univariate Tests Comparing Monastic, Apostolic, and Evangelical Congregations

Dimensions of Conversion	Hypoth MS	Error MS	F
Moral Conversion	257.57	75.53	3.41
Intellectual Conversion	321.05	86.22	3.72
Religious Conversion	230.32	56.16	4.10

The mean scores and standard deviation scores for the types of congregations and the three dimensions of conversion are presented in Table XIII on page 91. One hundred-forty five cases were analyzed. Of these 145 cases, there were:

110 respondents from apostolic congregations,
13 from monastic congregations, and
22 from evangelical congregations.

A Scheffe Post Hoc was done for each conversion variable, but no group differences were found for any of the three variables of conversion at the .05 level.

Table XIII: Means and Standard Deviation Scores for the Three types of Congregations and the Three Dimensions of Conversion

Dimensions of Conversion	Type of Congregation	Mean Score	Standard Deviation
Religious Conversion	Apostolic	88.68	8.06
	Monastic	92.38	5.63
	Evangelical	93.09	4.90
Moral Conversion	Apostolic	75.60	9.05
	Monastic	80.23	7.28
	Evangelical	79.86	7.39
Intellectual Conversion	Apostolic	72.45	9.49
	Monastic	76.46	8.32
	Evangelical	77.81	8.68

Research Question Three

What is the most important concept or behavior for a novice to learn and integrate into her or his own life by the end of the novitiate?

Findings
In analyzing the responses to this question, Katie read through all the answers several times and examined them for similarity. Because more than one answer was given by some respondents, the responses totaled 232. The responses were expressed in a variety of ways, but Katie discovered that they could be differentiated adequately under 7 categories. The categories were: religious conversion; moral conversion; intellectual conversion; integrated conversion which contained aspects of all three dimensions of conversion; personal identity of the novice; community; and service or ministry.

The complete summation of these responses is found in Appendix C. An example of a statement from each category and the number of responses for that category are presented in Table XIV on page 92. The responses are presented in descending order.

**Table XIV: Important Elements of Learning for the Novice at
the Completion of the Novitiate**

Category	Responses	Example
Religious Conversion	87 (37%)	Realizes she is uniquely loved by God.
Integrated Conversion	38 (16%)	Demonstrates a balance between: contemplating and acting; knowing self, God, and others; and understanding decision making and discernment.
Community	28 (12%)	Able to relate to others and to appreciate the charism of the congregation.
Moral Conversion	26 (11%)	Assumes responsibility for personal decisions; can name, claim, and articulate feelings.
Intellectual Conversion	25 (10%)	Is open to learn other facets of truth.
Service or Ministry	15 (6%)	Sees herself as a person with a mission of service.
Personal Identity of the Novice	13 (5%)	Is aware of own human strengths and weaknesses.

In describing the most important concept or behavior for a
novice to learn and integrate into his or her own life by the
end of the novitiate, the directors most frequently (37%)
described aspects of religious conversion. This data agreed
with and further validated the quantitative statistics which also
showed religious conversion being emphasized more than
moral or intellectual conversion in novitiate programs.

In addition, phrases and sentences which described all three
dimensions of conversion comprised the next highest percentage (16%). While aspects of community were the third highest
percentage (12%), moral and intellectual conversion ranked a
close fourth (11%) and fifth (10%) respectively. In other

words, the concept of conversion was distinctly present in many of the directors' personal responses.

Chapter V discusses the general conclusions, the implications of these research results, and the need for further research.

Notes

1. Geoffrey Loftus and Elizabeth Loftus, *Essence of Statistics* (New York: Alfred A. Knopf, 1982) 312.

2. Marija J. Norusis, *SPSSX: Advanced Statistics Guide* (Chicago: McGraw-Hill Co., 1985) 203, 218.

3. Dennis Hinkle, William Wiersma and Stephen Jurs, *Applied Statistics for the Behavioral Sciences* (Boston: Houghton Mifflin Co., 1979) 85.

Chapter Five

Conclusions and Recommendations

The Second Vatican Council addressed the significance and future of religious life and articulated that an integral part of that future is the men and women who are today embracing the religious life. The Council clearly expressed that the renewal and future of each religious congregation depends most of all on the initial formation of the new members.[1] Because of the central place of the novitiate in religious life and the novice's learning that is intended to occur during this time, the necessity of a sound theological foundation for the novitiate could hardly be overstated.

This study was designed to assist congregations to plan and implement their novitiate programs based on a theological foundation. With this in mind, Katie utilized Bernard Lonergan's theology of conversion to study the behaviors expected of the novice by the novice director upon the completion of the novitiate. She examined these behaviors in light of the necessity of a sound theological foundation for the novitiate experience.

Utilizing a questionnaire, Katie described behaviors using the Lonergonian dimensions of intellectual, moral, and religious conversion to determine the degree of importance the novice director gave to each dimension of conversion. The study also determined if there was a significant difference among apostolic, monastic, and evangelical congregations relative to the dimension of conversion emphasized in the novitiate. The research specifically focused on the expectations of the novice by the novice director during the academic year 1987-1988 and included women and men novice directors who attended the National Congress of the Religious Formation Conference in October of that year.

Conclusions

The conclusions are presented in response to the three research questions.

Research Question One

Is there a significant difference among the dimensions of conversion (intellectual, moral, and religious) emphasized in novitiate programs?

The test results for the repeated measures analysis for the dimensions of conversion (moral, intellectual, and religious) were found to be significant. The mean and standard deviation scores presented in Table IX on page 88 and Table X on page 89 indicate that religious conversion is receiving greater emphasis than moral and intellectual conversion. In addition, moral conversion is being emphasized more than intellectual conversion in these novitiates.

There was also a significant difference in how the respondents scored comparatively on intellectual, moral, and religious conversion. Table XI on page 89 illustrates that each conversion was significantly different from the other two dimensions of conversion.

These findings coincide with Lonergan's theology of conversion. He believes that persons first respond to God's offer of love in religious conversion, and then they are led to moral conversion and finally to intellectual conversion. However, in essence, Lonergan explains that there is only one conversion because religious conversion forms the basis for intellectual and moral conversion.[2] God's gift of love is free and is not conditioned by the human knowledge of intellectual conversion or by the ethical behavior of moral conversion. Rather, this gift of God's love is the cause that leads people to seek knowledge of God and to choose what is truly good.[3] Religious conversion comprises the premise for moral and intellectual conversion because to be converted religiously is to give oneself up to God's love flooding the heart and to subordinate everything to that love.[4]

Consequently, religious conversion is foundational to the novitiate experience. God's love is the catalyst that will cause novices to wake up and be attentive, to wonder and be intelligent, to reflect and be realistic, to deliberate and be responsible.[5] Religious conversion will imbue the hearts of the novices with the energy to put forth the effort and to endure the challenges involved in undergoing and implementing moral and intellectual conversion.[6]

These findings on the emphasis of religious conversion in the novitiate also coincide with the principle purpose of religious formation which is to immerse novices in the experience of God and to help them gradually perfect this experience into their lives.[7] The dynamics of religious conversion will help to focus novices on their specific call to religious life. This increased awareness of their vocational call will be accompanied by a compelling and overriding need to seek out the person of Christ, to learn more about him, and to draw closer to him.[8]

Every authentic love relationship manifests this same need to be with the beloved. The fundamental formative movement of the novitiate must be to facilitate the novices' growing attachment to the person of Christ and to his manner of life. This developmental movement is congruent with the dynamics of religious conversion. Everything else that is offered in the novitiate should complement the novices' deepening relationship with Jesus Christ.[9]

Additionally, personal transcendence will be normative if novitiates are grounded in a theology of religious conversion.[10] Novices will experience an awakening that challenges them to be pushed and pulled beyond themselves. They will come to realize that their search is not primarily their quest for God, but rather God's quest of them. They will come to realize that they are most powerful in their surrender to God's unique and individual love for each of them. They will desire to respond to this conversion experience by a loving response manifested in a vowed commitment to the Lord.[11]

Research Question Two
Is there a significant difference among apostolic, monastic, and evangelical congregations relative to the dimension of conversion emphasized in the novitiate programs?

The test results for the multivariate analysis of variance were not found to be significant. This indicates that there is no significant difference among apostolic, monastic, and evangelical congregations and the dimension of conversion being emphasized in their novitiate programs.

However, while there was no significant difference when the three types of congregations were compared to one another in relationship to their emphasizing one dimension of conversion, Table XII on page 90 shows that the test results for the univariate analysis of variance were found to be significant. This finding indicates that one form of conversion is being emphasized in each of these types of congregations. When the mean scores and standard deviation scores for the types of congregations and the three dimensions of conversion are examined in Table XIII on page 91, religious conversion has the highest mean score in each type of congregation.

Although the characteristics of the monastic, apostolic, and evangelical congregations are very different, an interesting aspect of these findings is that the directors of these congregations still chose to emphasize the elements of religious conversion in their expectations of the novices. To reiterate the characteristics of these congregations, the monastic congregation is centered on contemplation and the praise of God. Their model is the hidden life of Jesus in Nazareth before his public life and the hermits of the desert of the Fourth Century. The apostolic congregation is centered in the concrete mission of service to the world, with the members in common solidarity for this mission. Their model is the life of the disciples after Jesus' Ascension. The evangelical congregation is centered on fellowship in a spirit of simplicity and benevolence, and on a radical witness to Christ and his gospel. Their model is the disciples with Jesus during his earthly life.[12] Although the description of each type of congregation is very different, their focus for the novitiate experience remains the same—religious conversion.

Perhaps the underlying ethos in each of these types of congregations is the directors' belief that the novices must experience themselves as called and uniquely loved by God and must respond to that love, all of which comprise the substance of religious conversion. Consequently, although the characteristics of each type of congregation are different, the novice directors from all three types of congregations seem to agree that fostering the novices' personal relationship with the Lord takes primary precedence in the novitiate experience.

Research Question Three
What is the most important concept or behavior for a novice to learn and integrate into her or his own life by the end of the novitiate?

There were 232 response calculated for this open-ended question. The summation of these responses is found in Appendix C.

The responses which described aspects of religious conversion had the highest percentage of 37% (Table XIV on page 92). This finding corresponded with the statistical data in Table IX that showed religious conversion having the highest mean (89.68) among the dimensions of conversion emphasized in the novitiate.

The category in Table XIV with the next highest percentage was integrated conversion (16%). These responses contained aspects of all three dimensions of conversion — religious, moral, and intellectual conversion. This corresponds with Lonergan's belief that, in essence, there is only one conversion because religious conversion forms the basis for and the impetus to moral and intellectual conversion.[13]

However, Lonergan stresses that even though there essentially is only one conversion, the authentic Christian strives for the fullness of all three dimensions — intellectual, moral, and religious conversion. Without intellectual conversion, persons tend to misapprehend not only the world mediated by meaning but also the word God has spoken within that world. Without moral conversion, persons tend to pursue not what is truly good but what is only personally satisfying. Without religious conversion, persons are radically desolate; they live without fully realizing God's unique love for them.[14]

An interesting note in the responses to this open-ended question in Table XIV was that the category — personal identity of the novice — had the lowest percentage (5%). This finding contrasted with the literature which stated that novices must be grounded in their personal identity to facilitate the novices' responses to the demands of assuming a congregational identity. This personal identity enables the novices to grow in self-knowledge, to act responsibly, and to make appropriate choices.[15]

A possible explanation for this low percentage in personal identity is the tension between individual needs and ministerial needs present in some of the novitiate models discussed in Chapter Two.[16] These various models—therapeutic, prophetic, ecclesial, decisional, and initiative—accept persons into novitiates at varying levels of personal maturity. Those novices who have a strong personal identity when they enter the novitiate will require less time and attention in developing and fostering their personal identity. In addition, novice directors struggle with not making the novitiate so individualistic that the experience loses its corporate identity within a religious congregation situated in the Church. These explanations may help to shed some light on the limited number of responses in the category of personal identity of the novice.

Discussion

This study was designed to assist congregations to plan and implement their novitiate programs based on a theological foundation. Because of the significant findings which demonstrated that aspects of conversion were being emphasized in the novitiate, Lonergan's notion of conversion offers a firm foundation for the experience.

Lonergan's theological foundation will prevent the novitiate experience from being grasped by a person, group, or movement within or outside a religious congregation and turned in all directions.[17] Such a theological foundation will offer a rootedness to the novitiate and will structure the decisions that are made regarding the regular functioning of the experience.

This theological foundation will assist novice directors to articulate clearly what behaviors they consider important for a novice to manifest at the completion of the novitiate. As a result of this study and the emphasis given to religious conversion by the directors, appropriate experiences that facilitate this dimension of conversion will need to be incorporated into novitiates.

Religious conversion will focus novices on their call to religious life and on their personal relationship with Jesus Christ, who is initiating this special invitation. Through this process of religious conversion, the Lord will transform the novices. Thus the novices will be able to articulate a vowed commitment that is distinguished by sufficient knowledge, personal responsibility, free will, and an intense love of Jesus Christ.

Since one of the most important elements of religious conversion is the person's deepening relationship with the Lord, the directors will need to give special attention to the ongoing development of the novices' prayer life. Personal and communal prayer affords the novices the time to develop their unique relationship with the Lord. To encourage this relationship, the directors could utilize scriptural references similar to those presented in Chapter Two in novitiate conferences and classes. Scriptural references illustrative of religious conversion could be offered to novices for their personal reflection. Then in dialogue with their directors, the novices could reflect on the presence or absence of these examples in their own lives. These comparisons could enable novices to grow in an awareness of the Lord's unique and unconditional love for each of them manifested in their personal salvation history. In addition to sacred scripture, the directors could utilize other stories, images, and metaphors descriptive of religious conversion in their conferences with the novices.

However, as previously discussed, religious conversion is primarily a free gift of a gracious God—an outpouring of God's gift of love into human hearts. Since this gift of love is freely given by God, neither the directors nor the novices can force this conversion to occur. Therefore, the directors need to facilitate the novices' willingness to be the clay in the hands of the Potter (Jer. 18:1-6). In other words, the directors need to facilitate the novices' openness to receive and respond to this gift of love. This necessitates that the novices embrace a posture of asceticism characterized by a docility that sees the Lord's loving care in the vicissitudes of each day. This asceti-cal posture will enable the novices to continually turn to the Lord who offers this gratuitous gift of love.

Once embraced by the novices, directors need to realize that religious conversion will be manifested not by a privatized spiritual life; but rather by the novices' turn toward the neigh-bor. Religious conversion will affect the novices' imagining, experiencing, understanding, judging, deciding, believing, and acting. This experience will enable the novices to become less concerned with self, better able to transcend themselves, and more concerned with sharing this gift of unconditional love. Consequently, it seems appropriate to give less structure to some novitiate experiences. Some flexibility of experiences could allow the novices the space to choose to make this turn toward the neighbor rather than the directors making this decision for them by planning all the ministerial activities. For example, the director could allow the novices the freedom to explore ministry opportunities to ascertain where the novices would like to serve rather than the director choosing the ministry locations.

Because they have fallen in love with God, the choices of the novices will make sense only in and through this love. The experience of being obsessed by this love will finely tune their senses to the needs of others. The effects of this outpouring of God's love will be manifested in the novices' increasing aware-ness that "it is only with the heart that one can see rightly; what is essential is invisible to the eye."[18]

Recommendations for Further Research

This study was designed to explore the necessity of a theologi-cal foundation for the novitiate experience in light of the behaviors expected of the novice by the novice director upon the completion of the novitiate experience. This study has answered some questions and has raised further queries. To address these additional questions, further research is needed. Some avenues for additional research are now presented.[19]

The literature explained that the directors should be adequately prepared for their role. Of all the internal ministries in religious congregations, formation directors are ranked among those who bear direct responsibility for shaping the future of religious life.[20] Consequently, these directors should have an understanding of scripture, theology, psychology, sociology, anthropology, and human biology.

These directors should also possess wisdom; knowledge which has been assimilated, not just knowledge which has been acquired. They need to be people of vision and imagination, alive to new developments and opportunities in the Church and society. They need to possess an inner coherence, strength, and conviction. A study could be done to determine whether the educational programs mentioned in this study by the novice directors (Table VII) actually help to inculcate and foster in the directors the qualifications articulated as essential for religious in this role.

The literature stated that Church law demands that the novitiate last for twelve months to be valid. A thorough and systematic initiation to the religious life demands an extended time period for recollection, prayer, study, and reflection. A study could be done to determine how program length affects the outcome of novitiate expectations since the responses in this study varied from a length of 9 months to a length of 2 years.

There was a large percentage (85.3%) of intercommunity collaboration reported by these directors (Table II). Intercommunity novitiate programs could be examined to assess their grounding in a theological foundation.

Most of the novice directors in this study have been engaged in this ministry for a period of 1 year to 6 years (Table III). A comparative study could be done to assess if there is a difference in the expectations of the director regarding the novice relative to the length of time the director has served in that role.

Additionally, the survey developed for this study could be administered to novices themselves and a comparative study could be accomplished using the directors' responses from this research.

Furthermore, this survey could be administered to administrators of religious congregations and a comparison made between the responses of the novice directors and the responses of the congregational administrators.

This survey could also be administered to directors of the temporary professed members to ascertain if they would expect the temporary professed to manifest more behaviors in the areas of moral and intellectual conversion. A comparative study could also be effected with the temporary professed themselves comparing their responses with those of their directors.

Using the same concept of a theological foundation for the novitiate, the elements of a different theology could form the basis for further research; for example, liberation theology, sacramental theology, etc.

Another area of research could be the development of a model to assist religious congregations to ascertain what theology would be an appropriate foundation for their novitiate. I would suggest beginning with the writings and constitutions of the congregation and using these documents as the data, to assess what are the recurring themes and concepts present in this material. Out of this assessment, a pattern of values important to the congregation should become evident. The theology which is supportive to and congruent with these values would probably be the one most appropriate to form the foundation for the novitiate experience for the given congregation. Using this framework, the theology arises from within the heart of the congregation rather than being arbitrarily chosen from outside the community.

The following questions on religious formation, theological foundations, and conversion could also form the basis for further research:

Which elements of maturity do you consider essential for the candidate to possess prior to admission to the novitiate experience?

Which elements of instruction for novices do you consider essential during the novitiate experience?

What qualities should the novice director possess? How do you support and encourage the development of these qualities in the novice director of your congregation?

What are you willing to do, what action are you willing to take to address the problems facing religious formation today?

Why is a theological foundation needed for the novitiate experience?

How could a theological foundation be helpful in other aspects of religious life?

Should the type of congregation (monastic, apostolic, evangelical) influence the initial formation program of a congregation? If yes, how?

Should the type of congregation (monastic, apostolic, evangelical) influence the ongoing formation program of a congregation? If yes, how?

Is the conversion experience present or absent in your congregation? Give examples to support your response.

Does your community primarily function from the world of immediacy or the world mediated by meaning? Give examples to support your response.

How do you allow yourself to progress to various levels of human knowing—levels of experiencing, understanding, believing, judging, and deciding?

What memories do you have of moments in your life when you acted as a morally authentic person? What feelings are associated with those moments? How are those memories affecting your present moral choices?

What actions have you taken in the past 6 months to educate and sensitize your conscience?

What have been the results of making a judgment of value with insufficient knowledge of the situation?

What have been the results of making a judgment of value with insufficient knowledge of the probable consequences?

How do you experience yourself as worthwhile and significant because of God's unconditional love for you?

Is there an experience of passion in your relationship with the Lord?

Does God's love affect all your human operations—imagining, experiencing, understanding, judging, deciding, believing, and acting?

In your relationship with God, how does the tension between God's immanence and transcendence affect your life?

How do you experience God's Spirit at work in others, at work in your daily life experiences?

Since a review of the literature on the material discussed in this study revealed little in the way of statistical information, it seems to be an area that is rich with research possibilities. Katie hopes that much more data will be forthcoming in the future.

Epilogue

Katie was perched once again in the top of the pine tree overlooking the Pacific Ocean. As she gazed upon the transparent, green water, Katie realized that her search had validated her earlier concerns—although the focus of each of those novitiate programs was important, they lacked a foundation that would provide them with a raison d'etre. Katie sensed some inner peace in the results of her quest. Bernard Lonergan's theology of conversion could indeed serve as a foundation for the novitiate and could offer the experience the structure that would keep the roots ensnarled around the Rock and embedded in the Earth. The Earth and Rock would then nourish the roots of the novitiate and would prevent the novitiate from being buffeted by the storms of a changing world. With this insight firmly established in her mind, Katie smiled contentedly to herself.

A fluffy, white cloud appeared on the otherwise radiant, diamond-blue sky and Katie felt a nudge in her peace-filled thoughts. Katie had learned from Bernard Lonergan the necessity of awe and wonder and the crucial imperative to continue to be attentive, to be intelligent, to be reasonable, to be responsible, and to be loving. She gazed down at the tree trunk once again and was reassured to see the roots still firmly embedded in the Rock and the Earth. Realizing her flight was unfinished, Katie flapped her wings, spread them out to grasp the wind currents, and soared into the distant horizon.

Notes

1. *Perfectae Caritatis*, #18. Tickerhoof, 58.

2. Lonergan, *Method* 238-243. Meynell, *The Theology of Bernard Lonergan* 17.

3. Lonergan, *Method* 240.

4. Dunne, 112-113.

5. Dunne, 108.

6. Meynell, *The Theology of Bernard Lonergan* 10.

7. "Contemplative Dimension of Religious Life," #17.

8. "Renovationis Causam," #4.

9. Molinari, 56.

10. Lonergan, *A Third Collection* 131.

11. *Perfectae Caritatis*, #5.

12. "Evangelical Life," 2. Walsh, 400. Aschenbrenner, 653-668.

13. Lonergan, *Method* 238-243. Meynell, *The Theology of Bernard Lonergan* 17.

14. Lonergan, *A Third Collection* 248.

15. "Renovationis Causam," #4. Faber, 64.

16. Lescher, 853-858. Moffett, 23-26.

17. Lonergan, "Grace After Faculty Psychology" 499.

18. Antoine de Saint-Exupery, *The Little Prince* (New York: Harcourt, Brace & World, 1943) 70.

19. Recent works that include some discussion on areas examined in this book include: V. Bailey Gillespie, *The Dynamics of Religious Conversion: Identity and Transformation* (Birmingham: Religious Education Press, 1991). Mary Jo Leddy, *Reweaving Religious Life* (Mystic, Conn.: Twenty-

Third Publications, 1990). Diarmuid O'Murchu, *Religious Life: A Prophetic Vision* (Notre Dame: Ave Maria Press, 1991).

20. Joel Giallanza, "Self-Underestimating Formation Personnel," *Human Development* 9 (1988): 6-9.

Appendix A

GONZAGA UNIVERSITY

DOCTORAL STUDIES IN EDUCATION

October 8, 1987

Dear Novice Directors:

Welcome to New Orleans! I hope your visit will be an enriching and enjoyable experience!

I am presently a student in the doctoral program at Gonzaga University in Spokane, Washington. In my recent past, I was novice director for six years of the formation program for the Southern province of my congregation, the Marianites of Holy Cross. As a part of my doctoral work, I am attempting to identify, by means of a survey, <u>some</u> of the behaviors that you would expect of your novices upon their completion of the novitiate experience.

I realize that religious formation begins prior to the novitiate and extends beyond the novitiate. Moreover, there is a limitation to any survey. Consequently, the statements address only a certain number of behaviors which you may or may not consider appropriate for a novice ready to make vows.

The survey is divided into two sections. The first section contains the statements which describe certain behaviors. The second section contains questions about demographic data. This demographic information will be used to analyze the statements in various ways and to describe the participants of the study.

I want to encourage your participation in this project. My long range goal is to facilitate the development and implementation of novitiate programs in religious congregations. I hope to disseminate the results at some future time. Meanwhile I ask your support and prayers in the completion of this project.

Many thanks for your cooperation in this endeavor! The Lord's blessings be upon you and your ministry in formation. Please turn to the next page which begins the actual survey.

In Holy Cross,

Kay Kinberger, msc

Mary Kay Kinberger, MSC
Gonzaga University
Doctoral Studies
Spokane, WA 99258-0001

PART I

This survey is designed to help determine which behaviors you consider important for a novice to manifest by the end of the novitiate.

Please note that the statements below contain **only** some of the possible behaviors that might be appropriate for a novice to manifest at the end of the novitiate. This list is **not** intended to be all-inclusive.

According to your opinion, rank the degree of importance that you would give to each of these behaviors.

Please use the number 1 through 7 to register your response.

#1-----------------------------#4-----------------------------#7
Of no   **Of average**   **Of great**
importance.   **importance.**   **importance.**

POTENTIAL NOVICE BEHAVIORS: RESPONSE:

1. Assumes responsibility for his/her
   own personal development.   _____

2. Seeks to know and understand self through
   his/her relations with others.   _____

3. Shows a listening and receptive spirit
   in prayer.   _____

4. Strives to adopt a value system which forms
   the basis of his/her decisions.   _____

5. Experiences education as an ongoing and
   self-correcting process of learning.   _____

6. Demonstrates a strong trust in God's
   unconditional love for him/her. _____

7. Reflects on various ethical systems in the
   development of his/her values. _____

8. Utilizes and appreciates his/her intellectual
   abilities. _____

9. Experiences self as loving and being loved
   by God. _____

10. Bases decisions primarily on values and not
    on his/her personal satisfaction. _____

11. Reflects on personal insights and assesses
    these insights to discover what is true in them. _____

12. Views intimate and loving relationships as
    needed for personal growth and development. _____

13. Discerns those feelings which impact his/her
    values and judgments. _____

14. Seeks to know and understand other religions. _____

15. Shows a willingness to deal with the ambivalent
    feelings normally present in love relationships. _____

16. Knows that moral conscience is developed
    over time. _____

17. Demonstrates confidence in his/her intellectual
    and rational processes. _____

18. Knows that love involves judging, deciding,
    and choosing to love another. _____

19. Discerns values in dialogue with self and
    others. _____

20. Sets goals and long-range plans for personal development. _____

21. Seeks to discover his/her true self in relationship with God. _____

22. Deals with his/her personal fears concerning the unknown. _____

23. Strives to understand the history and charism of his/her congregation. _____

24. Knows that God initiates and calls the person to a love relationship. _____

25. Owns his/her feelings and can constructively express these feelings to others. _____

26. Questions and reflects upon his/her daily life experiences. _____

27. Sees the necessity of growing more open and attentive to God's love for him/her. _____

28. Takes responsibility for the development of his/her own moral conscience. _____

29. Can sensitively ask questions about his/her congregations's response to the gospel. _____

30. Fosters mutual respect and interdependence in his/her relations with others. _____

31. Takes a personal stand on the values affirmed as important to self. _____

32. Demonstrates that a deep, personal and communal life is essential to a relationship with God. _____

33. Participates in various experiences and
    educational opportunities that will develop
    his/her feelings.   _____

34. Strives to increase his/her own knowledge
    and understanding of the world.   _____

35. Demonstrates a loving care for others.   _____

36. Carefully examines the values which
    he/she has adopted.   _____

37. Examines the meaning and relevance of
    Church teaching in his/her search for truth.   _____

38. Experiences self as worthwhile and signi-
    ficant because he/she exists in God's
    unconditional love.   _____

39. Views long-range planning as important for
    the development of his/her congregation.   _____

40. Reaches out beyond self to others because
    God has become the center of his/her life.   _____

In three to four sentences or through key words, please
describe what you consider the most important concept or
behavior for a novice to learn and integrate into his/her own
life by the end of the novitiate.

_____

_____

_____

PLEASE TURN TO PART II

PART II (Please circle the appropriate response.)

1. Type of Congregation:

   Apostolic   Monastic   Evangelical

2. Size of Congregation:

   0-150   601-900

   151-300   901-1200

   301-600   1201-plus

3. Gender of Congregation:

   Female   Male

4. Do you work as part of a novitiate team?

   Yes   No

5. Do your novices participate in any way in a joint community novitiate program:

   Inter-Community Program?   Intra-Federation Program?

   Yes   No   Yes   No

6. The geographic location of the novitiate program which you direct or assist in directing is: (Please fill-in the space.)
   Country: _____   State or Province: _____

7. The length of the novitiate program which you direct or assist in directing is: (Please write in the time.) _____

8. The type of housing for the novitiate program which you direct or assist in directing is:

At the central administration
(e.g., provincial house, priory, etc.)   _____

As a part of another house, but not
the central administration house   _____

As an autonomous novitiate house   _____

Other (please specify)   _____

9. The length of time you have been in formation work is:
   (Please write in the time in years.) _____

10. This year (1987-88) the **NUMBER** of people residing in
    the novitiate which you direct or assist in directing is:
    (Please write-in the NUMBER.)

    Number of perpetual professed   _____

    Number of temporary professed   _____

    Number of novices   _____

    Number of pre-novices or candidates   _____

11. This year (1987-88) the **AVERAGE AGES** of the people
    residing in the novitiate which you direct or assist in
    directing is:
    (Please write-in the AVERAGE AGE of each group.)

    Average age of perpetual professed   _____

    Average age of temporary professed   _____

    Average age of novices   _____

    Average age of pre-novices or
    candidates   _____

12. Please briefly describe the education and training which specifically prepared you for your role as novice director or directress:

_____

_____

13. What theological school or philosophical point of view forms the basis for your novitiate teaching?

_____

_____

Thanks so much for your time and effort in completing this survey! I greatly appreciate your cooperation! Please return your completed survey to one of the designated tables in the rear of the conference hall. Many blessings!

Appendix B

SPSS Data Plan

Column	SPSS Variable Description	SPSS Label
1 - 3	Respondent's ID	ID
4	Type of Congregation 1 = apostolic 2 = monastic 3 = evangelical	Type
5	Size of Total Congregation 1 = 0 - 150 2 = 151 - 300 3 = 301 - 600 4 = 601 - 900 5 = 901 - 1200 6 = 1201- plus	Size
6	Gender of Congregation 1 = female 2 = male	Sex
7	Part of Novitiate Team 1 = yes 2 = no	Team
8	Intercommunity Program 1 = yes 2 = no	ICP

SPSS Data Plan (continued)

Column	SPSS Variable Description	SPSS Label
9	Intrafederation Program 1 = yes 2 = no	IFP
10	Intraprovince Program 1 = yes 2 = no	IPP
11	Location 1 = US 2 = Canada 3 = Mexico 4 = Australia	Locat
12-13	Length of Program in Months	Length
14	Type of Housing 1 = Central administration house 2 = Part of another house 3 = Autonomous novitiate house 4 = Other	House
15-16	Length of Time in Novitiate Work in Years	Time
17-18	# of Perpetual Professed	Numpp
19-20	# of Temporary Professed	Numtp
21-22	# of Novices	Numnov
23-24	# of Candidates	Numcand
25-26	Average Age of Perpetual Professed	Agepp

SPSS Data Plan (continued)

Column	SPSSVariable Description	SPSS Label
27-28	Average Age of Temporary Professed	Agetp
29-30	Average Age of Novices	Agenov
31-32	Average Age of Candidates	Agecand
33-72	Statements describing behaviors ranked in order of importance 1 = of no importance 7 = of great importance	Q 1 to Q 40

Summary Matrix of the Design

Research Questions	Data Collected	Levels of Measure-ment	Data Analysis Techniques
Is there a significant difference among the dimensions of conversion empha-sized in the novitiate?	See Appendix B (SPSS Data Plan)	Interval	Repeated Measures
Is there a significant difference among apostolic, evangelical, and monastic congre-gations relative to the dimension of conver-sion emphasized in their novitiate programs?	See Appendix B (SPSS Data Plan)	Interval	Manova
What is the most important concept or behavior for a novice to learn and integrate into his/her own life by the end of the novitiate?	See Appendix C (Responses to open ended question on page 3 of the survey.)	Nominal	Summation of the responses to the open ended question on page 3 of the survey.

Appendix C

Responses to the Open-Ended Question on the Survey

What is the most important concept or behavior for a novice to learn and integrate into his/her life by the end of the novitiate?

These responses were classified into seven categories. The categories in descending order of occurrence were: religious conversion, integrated conversion, community, moral conversion, intellectual conversion, ministry or service, and the personal identity of the novice. The responses in each category are now presented.

Religious Conversion

1. Has a love relationship with God.

2. Has a deepening response to God's call.

3. Values the beauty of her own humanity in light of Jesus' humanity.

4. Is loved personally by God and lives this love in community.

5. Is loved and called by God.

6. Has a sense of who she is in herself and before God.

7. Sees prayer as essential, prayer moves to mission and ministry; is loved unconditionally by God.

8. Has a deep relationship with God, self-knowledge and self-acceptance.

9. Relates his style of prayer to his personality.

10. Is open to God and others.

11. Realizes God loves her; has a good sense of self and her gifts in the congregation.

12. Is uniquely loved by God; discovers God's presence in and through her brothers and sisters; discovers the implications of that love.

13. Has a disciplined prayer life.

14. Relates to Jesus as the center of her journey; values prayer and scripture; has a healthy interdependence in relationships.

15. Has a sense of God's invitation celebrated in prayer; is committed to personal growth, and to the joy and pain of relationships.

16. Has a growing relationship with God.

17. Has a balanced inner and outer life.

18. Integrates prayer life and values into the congregation with a view to going out to preach the word in mission.

19. Has a deepening friendship with God.

20. Realizes she is loved by God, her family, and the congregation.

21. Is a human being in love with God, loving God and neighbor.

22. Has a desire for prayer and a sense of balance in ministry, prayer, relationships, care of self, leisure; is open to God, self, others.

23. Is called and loved by God; trusts in God, self, and others, values both personal and communal prayer.

24. Integrates her relationship with God in prayer to her relationships in ministry and relationships in and out of community.

25. Demonstrates a prayer-contemplative attitude in action.

26. Sees God's love and self knowledge as leading to a sense of self acceptance, to openness, risk and vulnerability.

27. Wants to grow in love and knowledge of self, others, God.

28. Balances contemplation and action.

29. Has a viable relationship with God and is a reflective person.

30. Balances prayer, ministry, leisure.

31. Experiences self as a loving person; giving and receiving love; developing relationships.

32. Demonstrates the importance of daily and communal prayer; values who she is in reference to God's call.

33. Is called by God who is active in his life; discovers God in others.

34. Trusts in the unconditional love of God; goes out of self for others.

35. Experiences self as a gift from God, practices deep personal and communal prayer.

36. Has a reflective, contemplative stance.

37. Trusts in God, self, community; has solidarity and compassion for others.

38. Has a personal relationship with God based on daily experiences and honesty with feelings; other-centered and not me-centered.

39. Has a sense of being personally loved and called by God; reverences the "other;" manifests interdependence.

40. Demonstrates the importance of prayer in all of life.

41. Has a deep personal and communal prayer life.

42. Searches for God, and has a deep prayer life.

43. Is open to God, seeking God; prayer is a priority.

44. Is a compassionate woman of faith and prayer.

45. Values a personal and communal prayer life.

46. Trusts in God's call and providence; seeks God in prayer and solitude.

47. Develops her relationships with God and others.

48. Experiences self as being loved by God and reaches out in love to others.

49. Has a contemplative spirit that moves to action.

50. Works on the development of prayer life; conversion; refounding of the congregation.

51. Develops communication skills in relationships; sees prayer as communication with God and communication with others.

52. Participates in contemplative prayer and daily examen.

53. Is empowered to accept self and reach out to others because of her experience of God.

54. Realizes she is specially and uniquely loved by God; all else flows from this conviction.

55. Has fallen in love with Jesus, and desires to continue to develop that relationship.

56. Trusts in the Lord's love.

57. Has begun her journey of identity with Jesus.

58. Has a personal and communal prayer life.

59. Accepts God's unconditional love and shares that love with others.

60. Has a personal, intimate relationship with God and loves others out of this relationship.

61. Demonstrates God's unconditional love by experiencing self as loving and being loved by God and reaches out to others in a caring way.

62. Is able to discern God's will and to respond to that call; is continuing to develop listening prayer.

63. Develops own spirituality in context of congregation's spirituality.

64. Experiences God's love, self acceptance, self love; has a deepening relationship with Jesus; accepts uniqueness of others; shows interdependence in relationships.

65. Has God as the center of one's life.

66. Needs to know God's love; is open and flexible, ready to keep growing.

67. Is Christ-centered and other-centered; is prayerful; has good self esteem and human development.

68. Is convinced of her own call by God; good relationship with Jesus in prayer and solitude.

69. Is motivated to respond to God's call to profess vows, is comfortable with spiritual direction.

70. Is responsive to the loving call of God by living out the charism and by participating in personal and communal prayer.

71. Lives a Christ-centered life, faithful to the gospel.

72. Is developing a strong personal and communal spirituality rooted in the charism of the congregation.

73. Is open and honest in relating.

74. Desires to grow in prayer.

75. Is developing relationships that will enable her to share her own life story with the story of salvation.

76. Sees God as the prime mover and formator; sees her relationship with God and formation as an ongoing process.

77. Is called out of love and is able to respond to that love.

78. Is aware of God's presence and action within him or her in all situations.

79. Is developing a relationship with God which leads to an increased knowledge of self and of God.

80. Integrates a contemplative stance toward self, others, God and the world which will lead to being a co-creator with God and others.

81. Has compassion, understanding, and prayerfulness.

82. Has a prayerful and discerning heart; is accepting of differences in people, lifestyle, and ministry.

83. Has a personal relationship with God.

84. Is able to surrender to the Spirit and to respond to the joys and sorrows of living in a Spirit-filled way.

85. Has a personal experience of prayer; has appropriated the skills necessary for the vows.

86. Has a loving acceptance of self and others grounded in a realization of God's fidelity and love.

87. Has experienced being loved unconditionally by God, all else will follow.

88. Has self acceptance leading to acceptance of others; has a prayer life that leads to a deeper relationship with God.

Integrated Conversion

1. Integrates personal prayer life and values into community life and values with a view to going out to preach the word in mission.

2. Has experiences of God, is loved unconditionally and through this conversion is committed to grow through community, prayer, and apostolate in God's love for life; is growing into the charism, the values, and vision of the congregation.

3. Has a deepening foundation in prayer and relationship with God; then the newly professed will continue to grow in all other areas.

4. Experiences self as loving and being loved by God, while striving to understand the congregation and its charism and becoming discerning and deciding, willing to evangelize and be evangelized by the poor.

5. Has a better knowledge and inner esteem of self so that a love of God and others can start him/her on the life long journey of formation.

6. Has a sense of being called and loved by God, wanting to express this through service to others and manifests a desire to deepen this experience; also has an understanding of the charism of the community and how that fits with his own person.

7. Begins to integrate prayer, community living, and apostolic activity.

8. Is experiencing conversion: changes in concrete behaviors and attitudes from individual/cultural values to the values of Jesus and the gospel; has faith in God's daily presence and call in the sacramentality of everyday events, people, feelings, experiences; loves the Lord thus present.

9. Manifests a balance in the following: contemplation and action; knowing self/God/others; understanding decision making and discernment.

10. Has a balance between being an individual and being a community member; between personal growth and ministry activities.

11. Is committed to prayer, to understanding of the charism of the congregation, to an appreciation of community values.

12. Has come to experience and come to know God's unconditional love; realizes self-knowledge is an ongoing process, an ongoing conversion; has the ability to give of self to others in ministry; has the ability to live with questions and ambiguities, to be open to the Spirit at work in everyday life.

13. Loves self, God, others leading to service; has an awareness of one's values, truth, and their impact on others; knows, loves, appreciates self in relationship to others; sees love as a self-giving and positive value.

14. Integrates feelings, thoughts, relationships, ministry, prayer; realizes this is a life-long process.

15. Shares her life struggles, goodness in community; has deep biblical values; is radically transformed in Jesus; internalizes charism and values internationality; critiques cultures in light of gospel values.

16. Has a sense of God's love for her; relates to God through everyday life experiences; integrates community, prayer, leisure and demonstrates a balanced approach to them; is able to relate to a variety of people.

17. Challenges the limits he has set and is striving to become more open; practices being a learner in relationship to life and is aware of God's presence and action within him and in people, events, and things of life from the perspective of the congregational charism and mission.

18. Has a relationship with Jesus, and a relationship with community; is able to reflect on experiences of life, God and religious community.

19. Takes personal responsibility for growth in prayer, education and ministry; desires to build relationships in community for building the reign of God in mission.

20. Has a deepening personal relationship with God; is developing a sensitive, listening heart; is oriented toward continuing self knowledge, and knowledge of the congregation's charism.

21. Has a deepening relationship with Christ and all that entails—charism, understanding of constitutions, and a sense of mission.

22. Experiences God's love leading to gratitude and sense of mission; desires to serve all, especially the poor.

23. Has a sense of being called and a desire to pray; is generous in service; is motivated to self-growth; balances spiritual, communal, and apostolic life.

24. Realizes that personal value and self esteem lead to valuing others and appreciating differences of others; knows they have a contribution to make and are wanted and needed; knows they are loved, needed and called by God, the Church, the congregation, and the novice directors; knows the poor will lead to a re-understanding of the scriptures and nature of the kingdom and hence to their own liberation/salvation; realizes that prayer is a part of life, a part of who they are; knows that relationships and community will reveal God to them.

25. Is serious about religious formation in a community setting for the sake of mission and with the distinctiveness of the congregation's charism.

26. Has begun living the community charism; is growing in love with Jesus; is growing in personal responsibility; is growing in Christian, Catholic believer behaviors.

27. Is called by God Who loves her; sees God's love demonstrated through the charism of a particular religious community; realizes that the only constant is change and

as members of a community we strive to support each other through change.

28. Has a personal relationship with Jesus that affects prayer, decisions, and life; has a knowledge of one's self; is internalizing gospel values; is able to discern gospel choices.

29. Has come to know self as a way to know God; is reflective of life experiences in faith; is discerning of the gospel call on individual and societal levels; is grounded in tradition of the Church and the charism of the founder; is able to read the signs of the times in the mission and to respond with flexibility; is able to live in and create community and to live in mutual relations with the congregation in vowed life; has a desire and passion for the mission and for one's ongoing growth and development.

30. Has a genuine desire manifested in behavior to be imbued with the charism and spirit of the congregation; manifests evidence that they are going to be life giving to the congregation and the people they will be ministering to and with; has the capacity and desire to continue to grow, and to become radical.

31. Has potential and takes responsibility for continued growth; desires and is able to respond to ongoing conversion of heart; understands the importance of her primary relationship with God and the inter-relatedness of the world.

32. Has a reflective attitude towards the events of his life; is able to grow towards and have experienced the pain of living for others in community; is able to feel a sense of deep rootedness in Catholic values and Catholic tradition; has had one personal experience of the presence of Christ within him.

33. Has a rhythm of prayer in daily life and experiences prayer as of primary importance in developing her

relationship with God; has the ability to reflect on and integrate her experiences and involves others in this process; has a sense of charism and believes in it and sees how this is the motivator for mission (global awareness); sees the value of balance in her life; likes self at work and at play.

34. Is open and willing to learn and grow; has an appreciation, respect, love for the founder and the charism; is honest about who she is, is willing to deal with personal issues; is able to live and work in the congregation and for others.

35. Has a relatively healthy self-esteem; has a sense of her gifts and charism and how these connect with the charism of the congregation; is able to notice her feelings and the subsequent effects on self; is in relationship with others and with God.

36. Experiences God's love and care of her and others; knows the charism of the congregation and is able to ascertain that her charisms are in line with the congregation; is open to experiences of sharing with others spiritually and in daily tasks, stating hurts, feelings, joys, etc.

37. Has self knowledge and self acceptance upon which a sound spiritual life can be built; desires to grow toward fullness of life and the ability to reflect on life's experiences and challenges in relationship to that growth and to relate to a significant other; has had a core faith experience as a tool for discernment; is able to name and communicate what her experience is.

38. Experiences a balance in the following:
    1. action and contemplation;
    2. gospel values and daily living;
    3. personal identity and community living;
    4. personal growth and the development of the mission of the congregation.

Community

1. Experiences identity and intimacy within a particular community.

2. Shares in the congregation's charism.

3. Is able to relate to others and understands the charism of the congregation.

4. Can listen to and dialogue with the professed members of the congregation.

5. Accepts the congregation as unfinished and is willing to journey together.

6. Has a community spirit.

7. Has a love of the congregation.

8. Participates in the congregation.

9. Internalizes the story of the congregation and its charism and the dynamics of community.

10. Integrates the charism.

11. Has a sense of the congregation.

12. Realizes community exists not for its own sake but for the Church and the world; well-grounded in the community—its history, traditions, and way of life.

13. Is transformed by the congregational story.

14. Claims the community.

15. Is compassionate to self and others in community; is open to change and is receptive to criticism; is able to confront others.

16. Shares communal life.

17. Shows relatedness with community; has relational ability in community.

18. Has developed community living skills.

19. Demonstrates an ability to live community.

20. Shows deeper immersion in the Christian community and grasps the charism of the congregation.

21. Is connected to the community.

22. Has a good sense of the demands of community living.

23. Shows patience and acceptance of the weaknesses of self and others.

24. Demonstrates compassionate living and working with others; appreciates and integrates the congregation's story.

25. Shows love for congregational charism and heritage.

26. Has increased community relationships and consideration for others.

Moral Conversion

1. Has inner freedom and is willing to let go of his life plan and allow God to lead him.

2. Is accountable to self and others.

3. Can make decisions which are enhanced with theological reflection.

4. Is honest with self and others.

5. Feels good about the call to this congregation.

6. Values the community.

7. Values the charism.

8. Values her experiences and makes appropriate choices; deals with conflicts and is a reconciler.

9. Shares feelings; is willing to collaborate in decision making, and to forego personal preferences for growth of the community and the Church.

10. Is co-responsible with the members of the congregation; takes initiative and personal responsibility for life.

11. Is transformed by gospel values.

12. Is responsible and challenged to personal growth.

13. Is responsible for his own ongoing formation.

14. Is involved in ongoing personal development.

15. Values the charism of the congregation, interdependence in the congregation, and relationship to the Church.

16. Assumes responsibility for decisions.

17. Stresses gospel values.

18. Can make choices.

19. Can name, claim, and articulate feelings.

20. Is honest with self in relationships.

21. Takes personal responsibility for growth and development of self-esteem in response to God's timing.

22. Takes personal responsibility in development of self and values consistent with the gospel.

23. Takes personal responsibility for growth.

24. Has sufficient inner freedom to experience being called by God.

25. Values an intense spiritual formation.

Intellectual Conversion

1. Understands the charism of the congregation.

2. Knows and understands the charism of the congregation, the three vows, and community life.

3. Is growing in knowledge of self and God.

4. Is growing in knowledge of oneself and of God.

5. Understands the vows, the vowed commitment, and the rule.

6. Has knowledge outside of her own experience, thinks and realizes alternatives other than her own personal stance on issues.

7. Has knowledge of God through self-knowledge and reflection on experiences; understands community charism and oppressive structures of society.

8. Sees, recognizes, understands their own patterns.

9. Understands self and her relationship to God.

10. Knows who she is in relationship to God, self, and others.

11. Articulates his own personal truth.

12. Understands personal motivation and work vs. compulsive behavior.

13. Knows own gifts and limitations.

14. Is open to learn other facets of truth.

15. Understands self, history, and charism of the congregation; knows importance of growth of self, growth in relation to God and others; is able to reflect on personal experiences.

16. Understands self and her relationship to God and that love entails bringing that love to others.

17. Is able to learn about self, God's call, the balance between community and the individual, and sensitivity to the community.

18. Is open to learn from experiences, opinions, and the changing times.

19. Reflects on daily life experiences.

20. Understands the charism.

21. Understands his/her own faith journey and the mission of the Church in the world and life as a process.

22. Understands congregational charism and the vows.

23. Is able to question:
    Who I am before God?
    How can I serve the Church?
    Is this congregation's charism suited to my way of experiencing self as giving and receiving God's life?

24. Understands God's love and understands that daily prayer is essential.

Service

1. Loves people and the Church; has a deep sense of justice, of the poor and oppressed.

2. Sees mission as an expression of call and charism; sees the vows as enabling the mission.

3. Is a public person with a mission of service; is a corporate cultural representative more than being a good professional.

4. Is willing to participate in the mission of the congregation; is flexible.

5. Integrates through ministry—the constitutions, social issues, and the Church's response to these issues.

6. Is called to serve others.

7. Is confident of being sent by God.

8. Participates in the life of the Church; can collaborate with others in ministry.

9. Collaborates with others in ministry.

10. Is growing in her desire to be with people in ministry.

11. Has the capacity for service.

12. Views prayer as calling her to want to help make a better world.

13. Has a sense of mission, ministry, and service.

14. Puts his gifts at the service of others.

15. Sees kingdom as a verb which means interpersonal service to others.

Personal Identity of the Novice

1. Accepts self as unfinished.

2. Has self esteem.

3. Has a balanced sense of self.

4. Is growing in self esteem.

5. Is self sufficient.

6. Is patient with self growth; is able to seek assistance from others to enhance personal growth.

7. Has self identity that leads to discern her call to the congregation.

8. Is able to be the unique person she is called to be.

9. Is aware of human strengths and weaknesses and acceptance of others; can be without others in a growthful way.

10. Embraces one's own personal story.

11. Has self knowledge, self esteem, self love.

12. Has a sense of own sexuality.

13. Has self confidence and flexibility.

DATE DUE

HIGHSMITH 45-220